The Report of the
Task Force on Barriers to Women in the Public Service

BENEATH THE VENEER

VOLUME 4

ANNOTATED BIBLIOGRAPHY

Canadian Cataloguing in Publication Data
Canada. Task Force on Barriers to Women in the Public Service

Beneath the veneer : the report of the Task Force on Barriers to Women in
the Public Service

Issued also in French under title: Au-delà des apparences.
Contents: v. 1 Report and recommendations — v. 2 What the numbers
told us — v. 3 What the people told us — v. 4 Annotated bibliography.
Includes bibliographical references.

ISBN 0-660-13584-1
DSS cat. no. BT22-19/4-1990E

1. Women in the civil service — Canada. 2. Equal pay for equal work —
Canada. 3. Canada — Officials and employees. 4. Civil service — Canada.
5. Women — Employment — Canada. I. Title. II. Title: The report of the
Task Force on Barriers to Women in the Public Service.

JL111.W6.C32 1990   Vol. 4   354.71001'04   C90-098618-2 65/24

© Minister of Supply and Services Canada 1990

Available in Canada through
Associated Bookstores and other booksellers

or by mail from

Canadian Government Publishing Centre
Supply and Services Canada
Ottawa, Canada K1A 0S9

Catalogue No. BT22-19/4-1990E
ISBN 0-660-13584-1

Abella, R.S. *Royal Commission on Equality in Employment.*
Ottawa: Department of Supply and Services, October 1984.

The Commission had the mandate to inquire into the "most efficient,
effective and equitable means of promotir.g employment opportunities"
and "eliminating systematic discrimination" for four minority groups
including women, in certain Crown corporations and corporations
wholly owned by the federal government. The Commission considered
proposals to eliminate pre-employment and workplace barriers facing
the four designated groups as well as support systems required for
parents seeking employment. The discussion on the elimination of
workplace barriers focuses on the need for mandatory measures,
i.e., federal legislation, adequately supported by an enforcement
mechanism. Four regulatory models were developed. The report also
deals with contract compliance, seniority and equal pay for work of
equal value.

Adler, N. "Women in Management Worldwide," *International
Studies of Management and Organization*, vol. 16, fall-winter
1986-87: pp. 3-32.

The author reviews the situation of female managers across a range of
countries. While the number of women who work outside the home
is substantial in many countries, the number of women in management
is negligible. The constraints are similar although the relative importance of each appears to vary from country to country. Barriers are
both psychological and structural, i.e., legal, educational, cultural,
social and historical. The two fundamentally different assumptions or
models about the role of women in management are summarized.

Andrew, C., Coderre, C., and Denis, A. "Stop or Go: Reflections of
Women Managers on Factors Influencing their Career Development."
Women in Management Research Symposium., Mount Saint Vincent
University, Nova Scotia, 1988, pp. 3.37-3.44.

This paper discusses the barriers and facilitating mechanisms that
exist for women in a management career and is based on interviews
conducted with intermediate and senior women managers. Both structural barriers (proportion of women, access to training, job classifica-
tion systems) and attitudinal barriers (attitudes of colleagues) were
identified by the respondents.

Andrew, C., Coderre, C., et Denis, A., "Les études universitaires: un atout pour les femmes gestionnaires dans les grandes entreprises", *Gestion*, vol. 13, no. 2, mai 1988, p. 68-73.

Dans une recherche effectuée auprès de 214 femmes gestionnaires travaillant dans les secteurs public et privé au Québec et en Ontario, les auteures ont étudié les cheminements scolaires de ces gestionnaires et l'impact sur leur carrière. La formation universitaire pour les femmes est considérée comme une clef d'accès aux postes de gestion.

Andrew, C., Coderre, C., et Denis, A., en collaboration avec Nicole Lemire, "De quelques notions de carrière chez les femmes gestionnaires", *Les cahiers de l'A.C.F.A.S.*, juillet 1988, p. 97-117.

Les auteures ont tenté de chercher à connaître comment les femmes gestionnaires définissent leur carrière. Ce travail est basé sur des rencontres en 1985 avec 214 femmes cadres intermédiaires et supérieures du Québec et de l'Ontario qui travaillaient dans les fonctions publiques fédérales et provinciales ainsi que dans de grandes entreprises. Quoiqu'elles notent des différences entre les femmes oeuvrant dans le secteur privé et le secteur public, la vision uni-dimensionnelle de carrières ne correspond pas à leurs réalités ni à leurs attentes. Leur vie professionnelle avait suivi des cheminements complexes et elles tenaient à cette complexité comme un signe d'une qualité de vie. Mêmes celles qui avaient eu un cheminement de carrière conforme au modèle uni-dimensionnel refusaient d'interpreter leur cheminement de cette façon. Par ailleurs, la primauté de l'intérêt dans leur travail était une constante. Les auteures conclurent que si la notion de carrière est complexe en générale, elle l'est davantage pour les femmes. Il n'existe pas qu'une seule manière de faire carrière pour les femmes gestionnaires.

Andrew, C., Coderre, C., et Denis, A., "Les femmes cadres, leur vie publique — leur vie privée. Sommaire des données", Ottawa, Faculté des sciences sociales, 1986.

Cet article est le sommaire d'une étude qui comparait le cheminement de carrière de femmes cadres dans le secteur public et le secteur privé. On souligne l'importance pour la carrière d'une femme de "parrains" ou "marraines" et des réseaux de solidarité.

Armstrong, P., and Armstrong, H. *The Double Ghetto: Canadian Women and their Segregated Work*. Toronto: McClelland and Stewart, 1982.

Through a detailed examination of the work women do at home or on the job, this study shows that when a woman is not employed full-time as a housewife, she is usually confined to fulfilling a housewife or handmaiden function in business. This book also examines the validity of three arguments that justify this segregation: biological determinism, cultural ideology and economic materialism.

Asplund, G. *Women Managers: Changing Organizational Cultures*. Great Britain: John Wiley & Sons, 1988.

The author asks why there are so few women managers, and decision-makers; examines the differences between men's and women's careers and analyzes the concept of "organizational culture" and how women fit in. New organizational forms are inevitable the author argues and so are new leadership styles. Many of the examples or case studies are taken from Sweden.

Baron, A.S. "What Men Are Saying about Women in Business: A Decade Later." *Business Horizon*, vol. 32, no. 4, July-August 1989: pp. 51-53.

This short article compares the results of two surveys (1981 and 1988) on men's attitudes towards women in business. The author believes that there is more and more acceptance of women although on some issues, men are still very "cautious."

Baron, J.N., and Beilby, W. "Organizational Barriers to Gender Equality: Sex Segregation of Jobs and Opportunities." In Rossi, A.S., *Gender and the Life Course*. New York: Aldine Publishing Co., 1988: pp. 233-251.

This article demonstrates the persistence of gender stratification in a complex economy — namely the United States. Their research suggests that firms differ less in the extent of sex segregation than in the processes and structures that generate and sustain segregation. The authors discuss the implications of segregation for the careers of men and women and look at various policies/strategies aimed at achieving equity in the workplace. In terms of the policy implications of their study, the authors state bluntly that "high levels of segregation seem likely to persist if policymakers adopt a laissez-faire approach." There are no "natural" forces leading to a balanced sex ratio within organizations.

Bassett, I. *The Bassett Report: Career Success and Canadian Women.* Toronto: Collins Publishers, 1985.

Television journalist Isabel Bassett asks why more women have not moved into senior positions and attempts to analyze why they are held back and why they think they are being held back. She identifies both exterior and interior barriers — subtle social forces (such as corporate culture, tradition, discrimination) and women's own lower expectations and fear of risk. While recognizing the importance of government enacted legislation for employment equity for women, the author emphasizes that women themselves have to work for change including the socialization of their children. Sources include open-ended interviews with a cross section of men and women across Canada, a poll conducted by Martin Goldfarb and current literature on the subject.

Baudoux, C., "Demandées: directrices et femmes", *Gestion*, vol. 13, no. 1, février 1988, p. 57-62.

Contrairement à ce qui se produit dans le secteur privé, le taux de gestionnaires féminines en éducation décroit depuis 1960. Les résultats d'une étude basée sur un échantillon représentatif de directeurs et directrices d'écoles primaires et secondaires au Québec, amènent l'auteure à retenir deux hypothèses pour expliquer ce phénomène — soit celle de l'invisibilité des femmes (elles ne sont pas présentes ou ne prennent pas les décisions importantes et elles n'ont pas accès aux mêmes ressources du monde scolaire) et celle des rôles contradictoires qui sont confiés aux femmes gestionnaires.

Baudoux, C., "Des organisations et des femmes" dans Baudoux, C., et De La Durantaye, C.V., *La femme de l'organisation*, Québec, Presses de l'Université du Québec, 1988, p. 13-52.

Dans cet ouvrage, l'auteure tente d'expliquer le faible taux de féminisation des postes stratégiques des organisations. Deux types d'éléments explicatifs sont présentés pour expliquer ce "phénomène d'exclusion" — l'attitude des femmes elles-mêmes par l'entremise des stratégies qu'elles utilisent face à l'organisation et les caractéristiques propres de l'organisation, c'est-à-dire, la "culture patriarcale" de l'organisation qui, selon l'auteure, éloigne de façon systématique les femmes qui veulent accéder au pouvoir.

Bennett, J.E., and Loewe, P.M. *Women in Business: A Shocking Waste of Human Resources.* **A Financial Post Book, Toronto: Maclean-Hunter Limited, 1975.**

This book throws light on the lack of commitment of Canadian business to equal opportunity. Further, it emphasizes the dangers of discrimination and stereotypes by giving specific examples relating to occupational segregation and compensation. It also provides valuable hints for organizations that want to make themselves efficient in the process of providing equal opportunity. The findings are usually Canadian-specific, but often illustrates cases with the American experience.

Bergmann, B. "Does the Market for Women's Labor Need Fixing?" *Journal of Economic Perspectives,* **vol. 3. no. 1, 1989: pp. 43-60.**

The author reviews current evidence on the discrimination against women in the labour market and the consequences this has on their pay and status. Remedies are called for, it is argued and the merits and defects of two commonly proposed remedies — affirmative action and pay equity — are reviewed.

Bergmann, B. *The Economic Emergence of Women.* **New York: Basic Books Inc. Publishers, 1986.**

This book documents the "economic revolution" that has occurred as women entered the labour force in very large numbers and it analyzes the constraints and opportunities women face in today's labour market. The "root" of women's disadvantage, the author contends, is sex segregation on the job and the author provides statistical evidence to support the view that occupational segregation is due in large part to discrimination. The reasons for discrimination against women, the forms that it takes and the consequences of such are documented. Government intervention is advocated and a twelve-point policy agenda for future action is proposed.

Berman, M.A. "Talking Through the Glass Wall." *Across the Board*, July/August 1988; Friedman, D.E. "Why the Glass Ceiling?" *Across the Board*, July/August 1988; Friedman, D.E. "The Invisible Barrier to Women in Management." *Across the Board*, winter 1988.

These articles give reasons why women are being discriminated against. These reasons are either legitimate or due to stereotypes, in which case they are referred to as the "glass ceiling." Indicators are also given on how companies can help their female employees reduce the tensions of conciliating a family life with career responsibilities.

Bhatnagar, D. "Professional Women in Organizations: New Paradigms for Research and Action." *Sex Roles*, vol. 18., no. 5/6, March 1988: pp. 343-355.

Reviewing the research on some of the major issues encountered by professional women in the workplace (social isolation, nonavailability of mentors, tokenism, sex-role stereotyping and discrimination through under-rating and underpaying), the author indicates that the reasons for these problems are usually sought through either person-centred explanations or situation-specific explanations. This article suggests that viewing these issues as concerns of a sub-system of an organization rather than strictly as issues of concern to a subgroup and viewing the impact of such problems on the organization as a whole could lead to a problem-solving approach at the organizational level. Organizational strategies to overcome those problems could then be devised.

Bielby, D.D., and Beilby, W. "Women's and Men's Commitment to Paid Work and Family." *Women and Work*, ed. Gutek, B.A., Stromberg, A.H., and Larwood, L., vol. 3, spring 1988.

A literature review that presents three alternative perspectives of how individuals develop preferences for a particular balance of paid work and family activities. These commitments may differ from one sex to the other and have different implications depending on which model you select to analyze them. The authors also present a model that might synthesize the three other approaches.

Block, W., and Walker, M. "On Employment Equity." The Fraser Institute, Vancouver, *Focus* no. 17, 1985.

This critique of the Abella Report underlines the "unsatisfactory economic analysis employed," and argues that other alternatives to "employer discrimination" were not explored. The authors also argue that the Commission did not consider an important finding of previous Fraser Institute studies, namely, "that marital status and the unequal family, home and child-care responsibilities it engenders" is crucial in understanding male-female income differences. It is argued that legislation is a barrier and that the "voluntary forces" of the market rather than legislation should be utilized to bring about equality between men and women.

Blum, L., and Smith, V. "Women's Mobility in the Corporations: A Critique of the Politics of Optimism." *Signs, Journal of Women in Culture and Society*, vol. 13, no. 3, 1988: pp. 528-545.

Reviewing the limitations of the two most popular models of gender relations in the workplace (the organizational model and the individual personality model) the authors contend that the optimism that has resulted from the increase of women in executive and managerial occupations exaggerates both the actual extent of women's integration and the actual opportunities available in managerial ranks. A more comprehensive perspective, one that examines differences among women themselves and among different organizations, will provide a more realistic picture and by extension, more realistic strategies for women's mobility.

Brass, D.J. "Men's and Women's Networks: A Study of Interaction Patterns and Influence in an Organization." *Academy of Management Journal*, vol. 28, no. 2, 1985: pp. 327-343.

This study investigated the interaction patterns of men and women in an organization and the relationship of these patterns to (1) perceptions of influence, and (2) promotions to supervisory positions. Results indicated that individuals' positions in workflow and interaction networks relate strongly to measures of influence. Although women were rated as less influential than men, the two groups showed no difference on many measures. However, women were not well-integrated into men's networks including the organization's dominant coalition, and vice versa. Women whose immediate workgroups included both men and women were exceptions. A follow-up indicated that promotions were significantly related to centrality in departmental, men's, and dominant-coalition interaction networks.

Bremer, K., and Howe, D.A. "Strategies Used to Advance Women's Careers in the Public Service: Examples from Oregon." *Public Administration Review*, **Nov./Dec. 1988: pp. 957-961.**

This is a case study of seven public agencies in Oregon that had success in moving women into management positions. Twenty-three people from these agencies were interviewed on the change of the status of women in their organizations and on the factors they thought contributed to this change. Based on these interviews, the authors identified six key strategies including the importance of a strong management commitment to women's advancement, a high value on excellence and promoting from within if possible. According to the authors, their findings do not differ from those observed in the private sector.

Buckland, L. "Education and Training Opportunities: Equal Opportunities or Barriers to Employment?" *Research Studies of the Royal Commission on Equality in Employment*. **Ottawa: Department of Supply and Services, 1985, pp. 131-156.**

The author examines the relationship between education, training and equality in employment for the four target groups that were the subject of the Abella Commission. The relationship is complex — inequalities in education have their roots in the unequal nature of the social structure. However, in the case of women, the author indicates that even access to and attainment of higher education and training does not ensure equality of opportunity. The author reviews the barriers for women in education and training, discusses possible scenarios of the future and underlines the urgency for preparing disadvantaged minority groups including women for the future. She warns, however, that the pursuit of equality through education will not be effective unless the basic issues of the inequalities of condition and status are addressed.

The Bureau of National Affairs, *Work and Family: A Changing Dynamic*. Washington, D.C.: 1986.

This report explores the range of responses that are being studied and adopted by the public and private sectors and unions to meet the new needs of the changing American workplace. Information on more than 30 case studies on child care, alternative work schedules, employee assistance programs, parental leave and relocation assistance programs is included as well as a chapter on international trends and a section on labour management approaches. The question of who is responsible for accommodating these new realities of the workplace is also addressed.

Burshardt, S.C., and Allen, B. "Role Ambiguity in the Male/Female Protege Relationship." *Equal Opportunities International*, vol. 7, no. 2, 1988: pp. 5-8.

Mentorship, as an important element of career enhancement, is well documented the authors point out. However, the male mentor/female protege combination appears to be the most complex of mentoring relationships because, the authors argue, of the similarity between the cultural mating role and the mentoring role. This can lead to problems with peers and spouses. Such problems are unique to this type of mentoring and the authors suggest strategies to overcome possible difficulties.

Canada, Commission de la Fonction publique. *La femme dans la Fonction publique fédérale du Canada — Dix ans d'évolution*, Ottawa, 1985.

A l'occasion de l'Année internationale de la femme, la Commission présente un bilan de l'amélioration de la situation de la femme dans la fonction publique fédérale. Quoique les ministères fédéraux ont fait, selon la Commission, des progrès remarquables, l'objectif que les femmes soient representées de façon équitable à tous les niveaux, est loin d'être atteint. Le rapport énumère les programmes et services qui ont favorisé les changements et rappelle les mesures que la Commission a pris pour éliminer les obstacles au recrutement des femmes.

Canadian Advisory Council on the Status of Women. *On Employment Equity: A Brief to the Legislative Committee on Employment Equity (Bill C-62)*. Ottawa: December 1985.

A brief outlining the Council's position regarding the limitations of Bill C-62, the federal government's response to the Abella Commission. The Council's concerns centred on the coverage criteria, the definition of employment equity, the reporting criteria and enforcement mechanisms. As well, the Council outlined concerns it had with several other employment equity measures introduced by the federal government which would affect federal contractors, the public service and Crown corporations.

Cannings, K. "Managerial Promotion: The Effects of Socialization, Specialization and Gender." *Industrial and Labour Relations Review*, vol. 42, no. 1, October 1988: pp. 77-88.

The purpose of this study was to estimate the extent to which gender affects managerial career success by analyzing the rate of promotion among middle managers in a large Canadian corporation. Although such factors as childhood socialization, education and firm specific productivity had a significant impact on the probability of promotion, the author finds that even when these variables are held constant, gender influenced a manager's chances of promotion, women were not as likely as their male colleagues to be promoted.

Carsrud, A.L., Gaglio, C.M., and Olm, K.W. "Entrepreneurs-mentors Networks and Successful New Venture Development: An Exploratory Study." *American Journal of Small Business*, vol. 12, fall 1987: pp. 13-18.

The paper deals with the social context of entrepreneurship, specifically the effects of mentors and networks. Although the results are not empirically conclusive, the paper is important in demonstrating in one instance (and I [Editor Neil C. Churchill] suggest that this may hold in many others) that managerial beliefs appropriate to and substantiated by research in large organizations are not always relevant and, indeed, may even be dysfunctional in entrepreneurial situations.

The paper also highlights the need for research on personality traits, backgrounds, and experiences to be embedded in the organizational, economic, and social environment in which the entrepreneur operates if it is to be relevant to entrepreneurship.

Chaganti, R. "Management in Women-Owned Enterprises." *Journal of Small Business Management*, October 1986.

Women's management style is being analyzed in this article with respect to two models of strategic management. Findings emphasize the fact that successful women-owned enterprises resemble the entrepreneurial model, but that managerial styles may be more "feminine" among women entrepreneurs.

Chicha-Pontbriand, M.T., *Discrimination systémique — Fondement et méthodologie des programmes d'accès à l'égalité en emploi*, Cowansville (Québec) Les Editions Yvon Blais Inc., 1989.

Afin de combattre la discrimination systématique, l'auteure tente de démontrer par un approche pluridisciplinaire, qu'il est indispensable de dépasser le cadre étroit d'une entreprise ou d'un organisme. La discrimination face aux femmes (et d'autres groupes défavorisés) est de nature dynamique et l'interaction de certains variables (économiques, psychologiques, législatifs, etc...) contribuent à maintenir cette situation d'inégalité. L'auteure examine donc l'influence des pratiques de gestion du personnel, l'accès aux programmes de formation et le système d'éducation. A partir d'un portrait statistique de la situation d'inégalité des femmes (et des autres groupes cibles) sur le marché du travail, l'auteure définit la discrimination systémique et établit les conditions nécessaires d'un correctif systémique. L'outil essentiel selon l'auteure est l'analyse de disponibiité et la méthodologie à suivre pour estimer cette disponibilité est présentée de façon détaillée.

Chicha-Pontbriand, M.T., "Sommes-nous à la fine pointe?", *Avenir*, vol. 3, no. 1, janvier-février 1989, p. 29-31.

L'auteure souligne les facettes du problème de l'égalité en emploi et son étendu. Elle souligne la segrégation professionnelle des femmes et des hommes, l'inégalité des salaires, le travail précaire des femmes, l'influence des préjugés et des valeurs sur les pratiques d'emploi dans les entreprises et l'influence souvent négative de cet ensemble de facteurs sur le comportement des femmes. Deux moyens prévus par la charte québecoise pour assurer l'égalité en emploi sont résumés et leurs lacunes soulignées. Une approche "proactive" généralisée à l'ensemble des employeurs est préconisée.

Chusmir, L., and Durand, D. "The Female Factor." *Training and Development Journal*, vol. 41, no. 8, August 1987: pp. 32-37.

It is argued in this article that stereotypes and myths about female employees cause many organizations to under-utilize women. The authors attempt to "de bunk" some of the most commonly held stereotypes — women's high rate of absenteeism and their lack of commitment to their job — and offer advice to managers on steps, which can be taken, to help women remain a strong force in organizations.

Cohen, S.L., and Bunker, K.A. "Subtle Effects of Sex Role Stereotypes on Recruiters' Hiring Decision." *The Journal of Applied Psychology*, vol. 60, 1975: pp. 566-572.

A survey of male job recruiters was carried out to investigate the relevance of allegedly sex-oriented occupations to personnel selection decisions. The results showed discrimination at the initial stages of the job selection process (recruitment interview). This may only apply for positions with a sex-orientation or connotation incongruent with sexes.

Collins, A. "Why We're not Number One: A Position Paper from Canada's Top Corporate Women," *Canadian Business*, November 1988: p. 32.

This article, based on interviews with twelve female executives at the vice-president's level, provides an overview of some of the gender-based barriers these women have had to overcome to reach this level. Although the most overt barriers appear to have been reduced, invisible barriers are still there. The author concludes that numbers are important and that many more women in the senior levels of the corporate world are required so that they can be involved in defining the corporate culture.

Collins, E.G.C. "Managers and Lovers." *Harvard Business Review*, September-October 1983: pp. 142-153.

The author argues that love threatens the organization's stability, and she urges top management to view it in that light. Through four case histories, she shows how the threat manifests itself, how it plays itself out throughout various parts of the company, and what top managers must do to preserve the organization and ensure that top employees remain motivated to work toward that preservation.

Colwill, N.L., and Josephson, W. "Attitudes Toward Equal Opportunity in Employment: The Case of One Canadian Government Department." *Business Quarterly*, spring 1983: pp. 87-93.

This article is based on the results of a questionnaire sent to approximately 1,200 employees in one geographical area of a large Canadian government department. The objective of the survey was to get at employee attitudes including attitudes towards the department's EOW program and surrounding issues. More alike than different in their job satisfaction and career goals, men and women differed substantially on their attitudes toward women and work. Men were more likely to respond that women's careers were limited by their personal qualities (lack of natural ability, lack of interest in job advancement, lack of acceptance of responsibility or their inability to tolerate stress). Women, on the other hand, were more likely to respond that women's careers were limited by external factors (lack of encouragement to compete for better jobs in the department, lack of opportunity to train, lack of acceptance by coworkers and supervisors). However, these women did not want preferential programs. Bridging positions, upgrading through the use of developmental assignments and more frequent use of on-the-job training were preferred options. The authors conclude with recommendations for organizations wishing to undertake an equal opportunity program.

Colwill, N.L. "Fear of Success in Women: Organizational Reality or Psychological Mythology?" *Business Quarterly*, vol. 49, no. 3, fall 1984: pp. 20-21.

The author reviews Horner's concept of "fear of success" in women (first introduced in 1968) and the research that followed in the aftermath. Horner's conclusions, according to the author, are not borne out.

Colwill, N.L. "Men and Women in Organizations: Roles and Status, Stereotypes and Power." In *Working Women: Past, Present, Future*, ed. Koziara, K.S., Moskow, M.H., and Taner, L.D. Washington, D.C.: Bureau of National Affairs, 1987, pp. 97-117.

The author discusses sex-stereotyping in society and on the job and looks at the inter-relationships between sex roles, sex-stereotyping, status and power. A consistent feature of sex roles, the author contends, is the belief that women and "all things feminine have been seen as inferior to men and all things masculine" and therefore, the "organizational roles played by men have been the important work roles of (the) society...." Included is a review of how men and women are perceived and how these beliefs discriminate against women in certain job assignments and particularly in managerial positions. Stereotyping also influences the relative power of men and women on the job. A discussion of the different uses of power by men and women is included and anticipated trends in the focus of research on sex roles in the 1980s are identified.

Colwill, N.L., and Erhart, M. "Have Women Changed the Workplace?" *Business Quarterly*, **spring 1988.**

This article exposes the results of research on women in the workplace. It shows how things have changed and whether the change was due to women's movements or individual women's actions. Further, it tries to identify the effects of change with respect to co-operation, competition, and aggressiveness. Finally, the authors evaluate the speed of change and the factors of change.

Correa, Mary E. "Reactions to Women in Authority: The Impact of Gender on Learning in Group Relations Conferences." *The Journal of Applied Psychology*, **vol. 24, no. 3, 1988: pp. 219-234.**

The article looks at some of the myths and beliefs with respect to women for task leadership.

Coté, P. "Socialization." In *Men Changing: a Resource Manual for Men's Consciousness Raising*. **Ottawa: Alternative Futures Institute, 1984.**

The author shows how sexist socialization is initiated in childhood and continues far into adulthood. It also deals with roles fathers should play in child-raising.

Courtemanche, J., *La recherche sur les femmes cadres au Canada: une bibliographie annotée, 1980-1988*, **Montréal, Le Groupe Femmes, Gestion et Entreprises (sous la supervision de Diane Bégin), 1988.**

Ce recueil constitue un outil de référence à l'intention de personnes qui s'intérèssent à la problématique de la femme cadre au Canada. Une bibliographie annotée de 224 titres, anglais et français.

Coyle, A. "The Limits of Change: Local Government and Equal Opportunities for Women." *Public Administration*, vol. 67, no. 1, 1988: pp. 39-50.

This article examines the experience of equal opportunities (EO) policies adopted by local governments in Great Britain as they relate to women over the 1982-87 period. Women make up 60% of all local government employees but they are not evenly represented throughout the local government structure. They are overwhelmingly concentrated in low-paid, low-status jobs and under-represented as decision-makers even in those departments where women predominate. The author concludes that the EO policies have achieved limited results to date due to few resources, little managerial or political support and guidance, no implementation mechanisms or management accountability. While EO policies were developed within the existing relationships and structures of local governments, the author concludes that new strategies that emphasize "collective, organizational and structural change" will have to be developed in order that "new organizational structures, new cultures and new values" can emerge.

Crosby, F. "The Denial of Personal Discrimination." *American Behavioral Scientist*, vol. 27, no. 3: pp. 371-386.

Working women in one survey knew that women workers do not generally receive the rewards they deserve. But in most cases, the women appeared to imagine — quite erroneously — that they personally avoided sex discrimination. After documenting the basic phenomenon, the article discusses cognitive and emotional barriers to the acknowledgement of personal discrimination. Ways to surmount the barriers are discussed.

Cullen, D. "Career Barriers: Do We Need More Research?" *Women in Management Research Symposium*, Mount Saint Vincent University, Nova Scotia, 1988, pp. 3.28-3.36.

The study of career barriers for women has focused on the behaviour and struggle of individual women, rather than on the structure and nature of the organizations in which they are struggling. The author believes that future research on career barriers should focus on the characteristics of organizations, rather than on the characteristics that women need to succeed. The paper gives a selective overview of the individualist approach and explores some of its limits.

Dagg, A.I., and Thompson, P.J. *MisEducation: Women and Canadian Universities.* Toronto: OISE Press, 1988.

The authors' objectives are twofold — to depict the extent of sexual discrimination and the "incredible anti-women ambience" that exists in Canadian universities at all levels and to recommend how conditions could generally be improved. Despite public statements by universities on their role in ensuring that women are able to pursue careers as freely as men, the authors contend that the reality is quite different. Of particular interest are chapters one through four that deal primarily with students and the male orientation of curriculum, the marginalisation of women's studies, the general acceptance that male is better and the sex-segregated nature of university faculties. The authors believe that universities reinforce gender discrimination and their treatment of women students creates serious educational disadvantages for them.

David, H., *Femmes et emploi: le défi de l'égalité*, Québec, Presses de l'Université du Québec, 1986.

L'auteure adopte l'approche de la discrimination systémique. Elle soutient que l'organisation même du travail est un obstacle à l'égalité en emploi pour les femmes et que l'ensemble de pratiques souvent neutres en apparence, renforce la situation d'infériorité des femmes sur le marché du travail. L'auteure revoit en profondeur les législations adoptées depuis vingt ans au Canada et aux États-Unis et fait une évaluation critique de ces programmes. Les exemples soit tirées en grande partie de l'industrie manufacturière.

David, H., "La Portée des Luttes Contre la Discrimination Systématique et Pour L'Egalité Professionnelle en Emploi Dans La Conjoncture Actuelle", *Interventions Economiques*, no. 20-21, 1988, p. 191-204.

La notion des discrimination systémique est examinée et on compare cette approche avec celle des législations sur l'égalité professionnelle. En dernier lieu, l'auteure examine les limites de ces stratégies pour assurer l'égalité en emploi aux femmes.

Davidson, M.J., and Cooper, C.L. "The Pressures on Women Managers." *Management Decision*, vol. 25, 1987: pp. 56-63.

Women managers have to cope with greater pressures than men managers. If employers recognized and tackled this both women and men managers could do their jobs more effectively. The article deals with these issues and provides some suggestions on how government and employers could deal with these added pressures.

Davidson, M., and Cooper, G. "She Needs a Wife: Problems of Women Managers." *Leadership and Organization Development Journal,* **vol. 5, no. 3, 1984: pp. 3-30.**

This monograph is based on a large scale study of British managers in the private sector and investigates the problems and pressures of female managers in contrast to male managers. The results strongly suggest, the author argues, that women managers experience higher stress levels because they are faced with additional pressures (both from work and the external environment) not experienced by their male counterparts. Organizational and policy changes are included and the training implications of the results of this study are discussed.

Deaux, K. "Self Evaluation of Male and Female Managers." *Sex Roles,* **vol. 5, no. 5, 1979.**

Two separate samples of males and females holding first-level management positions in U.S. organizations completed questionnaires that asked for self-evaluation on a number of job-related characteristics and for attributions of causality for successful and unsuccessful job experiences. In support of previous research, results indicated that males evaluated their performance more favourably than did women, and rated themselves as having more ability and greater intelligence. Men also saw ability as more responsible for their success than did women, but the sexes did not differ in attributions to luck, effort, or task. Implications for equal opportunity and potential for change are considered.

Devanna, M. "Women in Management: Progress and Promise." *Human Resource Management,* **vol. 26, no. 4, 1987: pp. 469-481.**

Although education and changes in attitudes and values have enabled women to gain access to career tracks that were previously closed to them, the current area of concern is the slow progress of women once they enter large organizations. The author looks at the "organization process" to see if it is what women do that results in their slower progress or if it is gender-linked behaviour (cultural blinders) that those who hire and promote carry with them that determines career progress. The link between equity and motivation is also examined. She concludes by briefly outlining what organizations can do to foster change in how men and women relate to each other. Employers need to link managerial performance to equity goals, provide team building, help to forge mixed gender groups and to develop sensitivity to situations that cause men to resent women.

Devanna, M. *Male/Female Careers — The First Decade: A Study of MBAs.* **Centre for Research in Career Development, Columbia University, Graduate School of Business, 1984.**

The objective of this study was to determine whether wage differences existed between men and women who had the same backgrounds and qualifications and if there were differences, to attempt to explain them. The career patterns of a group of 90 male and female MBA graduates over a ten-year span were examined through a questionnaire. The data indicated that at the entry level there was no salary differential but that ten years later, women had gone from parity to a situation where they were making almost 20% less than the males. After examining other variables such as motivation, social experiences (marriage and children), sector and area worked, the author concluded that the major impediments to equal pay for men and women of equal qualifications and background were societal and organizational in nature.

Dipboye, R.L. **"Problems and Progress of Women in Management."** *Working Women: Past, Present, Future,* **ed. Koziara, K.S., Moskow, M.H., and Tanner, L.D. Washington, D.C.: Bureau of National Affairs, 1987: pp. 118-153.**

There is little doubt, the author contends, that the status of women in management has improved dramatically over the past two decades. However, management is still a "male domain" and the author offers little hope for any change in the immediate future. The barriers have changed — they are more complex and subtle but nevertheless they remain very real. Sex-stereotyping is a "primary roadblock" and women who aspire to managerial careers may encounter barriers from "gate-keepers" (for example, personnel officers, corporate recruiters) and the instruments they use to assess managerial talent. Once hired, women face other barriers that limit their advancement — such as exclusion from informal relationships with male peers, biases in job assignments and performance evaluations, a lack of mentors, inequitable compensation, sexual harassment and greater conflicts between work and family roles. Commonly used strategies and remedies to reduce these barriers are also briefly described.

Dubno, P. "Attidudes Towards Women Executives: A Longitudinal Approach." *Academy of Management Journal*, vol. 28, no. 1, March 1985: pp. 235-239.

The purpose of this research was to measure attitudes toward women executives of MBA students over an eight-year period (1975-83). Since previous research had shown that a strong relationship exists between attitudes and behaviour, studying attitudes towards women in management could help to explain their lack of progress in terms of position and salary. The results show that over this period, male MBA students retained consistently negative attitudes toward women as managers while female students were consistently positive. As well, the men were significantly more negative than the women were positive.

Dussault, G., "Différences de rémunération entre hommes et femmes", *Le marché du travail*, vol. 7, no. 7, Québec, juillet 1986, p. 66-71.

Dans ce texte, deux thèses qui tentent d'expliquer les différences de rémunération entre hommes et femmes sont analysées — la théorie du capital humain qui n'admet pas la discrimination et la thése de segrégation professionnelle, qui selon l'auteure tient mieux compte des écarts de salaire entre hommes et femmes. Les résultats d'une recherche comparant les conditions de travail (organisation du travail, promotions, progression et niveaux de salaires, assignation des postes) offertes à des employés de bureau de huit grandes entreprises de la région de Montréal vérifient, selon l'auteure, l'hypothèse que "les conditions de travail dépendent du sexe de la main d'oeuvre et non de la nature des postes occupés". Les valeurs sociales et la division des roles dans la famille influencent toujours la perception que les employeurs ont des roles féminins et masculins et par conséquence, la différenciation des échelles de salaires sur le marché.

Eberts, R.W., and Stone, J.A. "Male-female Differences in Promotions: EEO in Public Education." *The Journal of Human Resources*, vol. 20, no. 4, 1985: pp. 504-521.

The authors examine discrimination in promotions, more specifically, the gender differences in promotions to administrative positions in elementary and secondary public schools in the states of Oregon and New York. Based upon longitudinal data, the authors conclude that significant discrimination found in the early 1970s had declined considerably by the late 1970s and the enforcement of the federal equal opportunity legislation had contributed to the decline.

Ehrlich, E. "The Mommy Track." *Business Week*, March 20, 1989: pp. 126-134.

The author discusses the difficulties women face in attempting to balance career goals and motherhood and identifies how some large corporations have had to become more flexible in order to keep some of their best women. Alternative career paths, extended leaves, flexible scheduling, job sharing and telecommuting have led to a "mommy track," seen by some as a blessing but by others as a separate, unequal track that will permanently and negatively affect women's careers. Rather, some argue, the nature of corporate careers should change and both men and women should be supported in their need for child care. The challenge for employers, according to the author, will be their ability to provide both men and women with options and support for family life while contributing to the organization.

Eihler, M. "Applying Equality to Employment." *Research Studies of the Royal Commission on Equality in Employment*. Ottawa: Department of Supply and Services, 1985, pp. 207-212.

The author reviews the current state of inequality between men and women in employment and describes three different models of what equality in employment might mean (a) the proportionate representation model, (b) the equal opportunity model and (c) the equal rewards model. The third model is developed in some detail and involves creating a "woman-friendly" environment to the same degree to which environments are generally geared to men. The components of such an environment include non-sexist job entry requirements, moving women in cohorts rather than as individuals into positions formerly occupied by men, purchasing equipment that is equally suitable for all employees, the recognition and accommodation of the family responsibilities of all employees and flexible hours. Possible policy initiatives for achieving equality in employment are also included and are based on an incentive structure as opposed to penalties.

Epstein, C. *Deceptive Distinctions: Sex, Gender and the Social Order.* New Haven: Yale University Press.

The focus of this book is the changing roles of men and women in North American society over the last two decades. The author maintains that the basic differences between men and women are more superficial than we have been led to believe and that these differences are created and maintained by social forces and not biological forces. Chapter 7, on the Structure of Work and the Economic Pyramid, is of particular relevance here. The author reviews current theories that attempt to explain the sexual division of labour — the theory of socialization, the human capital theory, social structural analysis and theories of discrimination. The cause of occupational segregation is not found in any one theory, the author contends, but rather is found in a "combination of factors such as employee discrimination, women's choices, family pressures and public policy." The subtle informal barriers to the hiring and promotion of women in the workplace are also reviewed and the importance of networks, mentors and access to those with power are underlined.

Fagenson, E.A. "Women's Work Orientation: Something Old, Something New." *Group and Organization Studies*, vol. 11, nos. 1-2, March-June 1986: pp. 75-100.

The purpose of this research was to test two competing theories regarding why women are disproportionately represented in lower-level corporate jobs. The person-centred perspective argues that women's orientations are contrary to the demands of senior management jobs and that their attitudes and behavioural patterns in organizations are inappropriate. On the other hand, the organization centred view argues that individuals' positions in the hierarchy will shape their attitudes — that is, the higher the position, the more "top-management" focused individuals will be. Because women occupy most of the lower-level jobs in organizations, they have developed anti-success orientations in response to these jobs and their work environments. Using a two-page survey, women attending a conference on business in New York City were questioned on their orientations towards careers, organizations, jobs and subordinates taking into account their organizational level. The author concludes that the results support the organization-centred perspective and that the person-centred approach was not supported. The limitations of this study and the implications of the findings are also discussed.

Falconnet, G., et Lefaucheur, N., *La Fabrication des Mâles*, **Coll. Points Actuels, Ed. du Seuil, 1975.**

Les auteurs montrent dans cet ouvrage comment les hommes d'aujour-d'hui se représentent leur rôle, comment ils ont acquis leurs idées "personnelles" sur les femmes, la famille et le travail.

Falkenberg, L. "The Perceptions of Women Working in Male Dominated Professions." *Canadian Journal of Administrative Sciences*, **vol. 5, no. 2, June 1988: pp. 77-84.**

This study attempted to determine if there were differences in the perceptions of young, nonsupervisory male and female professionals in male dominated professions. Four hypotheses were tested — and only two were supported. Women felt that it was assumed that they had greater split loyalties between home and work and they indicated that they had to spend greater efforts to establish their status and authority than their male peers.

Feldberg, R., and Kohen, J. "Family Life in an Antifamily Setting." *Woman in a Man-made World: A Socioeconomic Handbook*, **ed. Glazer-Malbin, N., Youngleson Waehrer, H.. Chicago: Rand McNally, 1977.**

This article shows how the personal ideology of a family is dependent on external organizations. This in turn, leads to increasing difficulties for family members to be an emotional unit.

Ferguson, K.E. *The Feminist Case Against Bureaucracy.* **Series** *Women in the Political Economy*, **ed., R.J. Steinberg. Philadelphia: Temple University Press, 1984.**

This radical feminist book pursues three objectives: first, clarify the structures and processes of power in bureaucratic societies and their effects on the individual. Second, offer a basis for opposition through political resistance. Finally, suggest an alternative non-bureaucratic approach to the problem of organizations.

Ferrieux, E., et Guigon, C., "30–40 ans: Elles Veulent Toutes des Bébés, *Le Point*", 23 janvier 1989, p. 66-71.

Dans cet article, les auteurs montrent que le désir d'avoir des enfants a envahi la génération des 30–40 ans. Ces femmes veulent pouponner, mais cependant pas à n'importe quel prix. Elles programment leur grossesse selon leur planning professionnel.

Fitoussi, M., "Le ras-le-bol des Superwomen", *Psychologies*, janvier 1988, no. 50, p. 14-19.

Article humoristique sur la "superwoman" face à l'ultime obstacle de la femme au travail — la grossesse — et comment la vivre au bureau avec ces collègues, le retour au travail et les pressions additionelles qu'occasionnent les enfants sur la carrière d'une femme.

Fitzgerald, P.A. *Women Executives: A Canadian Profile.* ASAC — Policy, 1983, Conference Proceedings, ed. Baetz, M. University of British Columbia, 1983.

This article presents the results of a survey on Canadian women executives. It focuses on demographic features, compensation packages, career progress and satisfaction. It also provides information on career continuity, time management, work content and mobility.

Fox, B.J., and Fox, J. "Occupational Gender Segregation of the Canadian Labour Force, 1931-1981." *Canadian Review of Sociology and Anthropology*, vol. 24, no. 3, August 1987: pp. 374-397.

The article looks at gender segregation in the Canadian labour force and its effects on the working lives of women and men.

Fraker, S. "Why Women Aren't Getting To the Top." *Fortune*, vol. 109, no. 8, April 16, 1984: pp. 40-45.

The author attempts to discover why, in spite of impressive progress at the entry level and in middle management in America's largest corporations, women are having trouble breaking into senior managment. The reasons are elusive and sometimes difficult to identify. There are subtle barriers such as the comfort level — looking for managers with whom one is "comfortable," giving the best assignments to men and not giving women managers the same kind of constructive criticism that men receive. Other barriers include the perceived management style of women and the assumption that women with children aren't free to take on special tasks or travel. The question of "critical mass" is also briefly dealt with — studies have shown that while overt resistance drops quickly after the first few women become managers, it seems to pick up again as the number of women managers reaches 15%. Consistent and clear support for women managers from senior management is clearly needed and the author concludes with suggestions regarding what employers can do to open the executive ranks to women. Flexibility, revised personnel policies, rewarding managers for developing talent and vigilantly supervising the process are recommended.

Franklin, D., and Sweeney, J. "Women and Corporate Power." *Women, Power and Policy — Toward the Year 2000*, **2nd edition, ed. Boneparth, E., and Stoper, E. Exeter: Pergamon Books Inc., 1988: pp. 48-65.**

The authors examine the problems women managers and clerical workers encounter participating in and influencing corporate life. Two paradigms that are currently in vogue when trying to explain why women fall short of reaching the top are reviewed — the person-centred and the situation-centred paradigm — and the implications of each in terms of what needs to change before women can achieve full equality are discussed. The paradigms, alone or together, provide an insufficient explanation for the gender inequities that currently exist in American corporations and in fact the authors argue, the values they promote could be counter-productive in a world that is based on a service/information economy and one where labour markets are tight. Work and organizations must be looked at in new ways, the authors contend and they propose a new type of organization — the metanoic organization (the term denotes "a reawakening of intuition and vision") where they anticipate that women and the skills they bring could thrive and develop to the benefit of both organizations and women.

Friedman, D.E. "Why the Glass Ceiling?" *Across the Board*, **July-August 1988: pp. 33-37.**

The author reviews some of the barriers women moving up the career ladder face and discusses in particular the difficulties of reconciling work and family. Efforts to explain women's slow progress have, according to the author, "overlooked, underestimated and misinterpreted family factors" and argues that employers could do much for both male and female employees by developing policies and work environments that are supportive of family needs. Examples of supportive policies are included.

Friedman, D.E. "The Invisible Barrier to Women in Business." *Across the Board (Inside Guide)*, winter 1988: pp. 75-79.

The article looks at the role of the corporation in encouraging an optimistic future for male and female employees alike by developing policies and work environments that support family needs. The author highlights some of the more innovative efforts by some leading corporations in this field.

Gallese, L.R. "Corporate Women On the Move." *Business Month*, April 1989: pp. 31-36.

Level entry jobs and middle management jobs now appear to be quite readily available to women. However, the author argues, the barriers at the senior level, particularly in the line jobs, are still holding "firm." In fact, the author anticipates that these barriers won't disappear until the end of the next decade when the demographic shift which is currently impacting on entry and middle rank positions makes its influence felt on the upper levels. Isolated at work, not knowing how to use mentors, having to prove themselves constantly and being kept out of senior-level jobs because of "prejudice against powerful women," most women are consigned to a "velvet ghetto" where jobs pay well but don't lead to the top job.

Glazer-Malbin, N., and Youngelson Waehrer, H. ed. *Woman in a Man-made World: A Socioeconomic Handbook*. Chicago: Rand McNally, 1977.

This book is a regroupment of articles on gender roles differentiation, sex-differences, myths about women. It also gives specific examples of women's situation in China, Sweden, etc.

Glazer-Malbin, N. "Housework: A Review Essay." In *Woman in a Man-made World: A Socioeconomic Handbook*. Chicago: Rand McNally, 1977.

The author attacks here the myth according to which "women do not work in the home" and shows how the monetary value of housework could be taken into consideration.

Glazer-Malbin, N. "The Subjection of Women: Introduction." In *Woman in a Man-made World: A Socioeconomic Handbook*. Chicago: Rand McNally, 1977.

Glazer reviews, in this introduction, the literature written on sex-differences, gender roles, the minority status of women and the cast and class status of women. She further explains how socialization or economic conditions influence the woman's position in society.

Gregory, A. "Where Are We Coming From and Where Are We Going? Theoretical, Research and Methodological Perspectives on Women in Management." *Women in Management Research Symposium*, Mount Saint Vincent University, Nova Scotia, 1988: pp. 1.1-1.15.

This paper reviews the existing literature on aspects of gender differences and gender stereotyping. The impacts of these were considered in light of the workplace. Following each sectional review of literature are suggestions for future research directions that would contribute to a deeper understanding of women in management.

Grondin, D. "Research, Myths and Expectations: New Challenges for Management Educators." *Women in Management Research Symposium*, Mount Saint Vincent University, Nova Scotia, 1988, pp. 4.1-4.6.

During the late 1970s and early 1980s unprecedented numbers of women attempted to "reach the top" of corporate hierarchies. This paper examines three factors that have handicapped educators in preparing these women to meet this objective. The three factors are (1) the lack of casual explanations for both the success and failures of women executives, (2) the many myths still held by many women, and (3) the expectations women have with respect to corporate behaviour and opportunities. The article also discusses the impact of these factors on research in management education.

Gubbels, R., *Le Travail au Féminin*, ed. Marabout, 1967.

Quoiqu'un peu vieux, cet ouvrage passe en revue les composantes essentielles du travail féminin, détruisant un certain nombre de stéréotypes et montrant les avantages et inconvénients relatifs de palliatifs tel l'emploi à temps partiel.

Gutek, B.A. "Sex Segregation and Women at Work: A Selective Review." *Applied Psychology: An International Review*, vol. 37, no. 2, 1988: pp. 103-120.

This is a review of the literature (almost exclusively American) that covers several topics including problems for women in the workplace. Among these are sex-role spillover (the carry-over of expectations about sex roles to the job), short career ladders, tokenism and its implications. A common theme throughout the discussion is the sex-segregated nature of work.

Gwartney-Gibbs, P.A. "Women's Work Experience and the 'Rusty Skills' Hypothesis." in *Women and Work*, ed. Gutek, B.A., Stromberg, A.H., and Larwood, L., vol. 3, spring 1988.

This research contrasts two ways of examining lifetime work experience in relation to earnings: as characteristics and as length. The author challenges the notion that employment discontinuity is penalized in later earnings. Rather, she supports the hypothesis that, net of time spent out the labour force, intermittency is a rational strategy for maintaining work skills and should be considered by policy makers.

Haccoun, R.R. "Another Myth Goes Poof!" Canadian Banker, vol. 95, no. 3, May-June 1988: pp. 54-58.

The article deals with the prevalent belief that women have higher absence rates than men. The study revealed that the average relationship between gender and absence levels is very low. Gender explains a trivial amount of absence.

Hardesty, S., and Jacobs, N. *Success and Betrayal — The Crisis of Women in Corporate America*. New York: Simon and Schuster, Inc., 1987.

This book deals with the myths and realities of women who want to reach beyond middle management. Based on interviews with both women and men in large American corporations, the authors describe a life cycle for women managers — that is a series of "landings" or "evaluative points" specific to women's careers. They also discuss the invisible barriers that are part of the corporate culture and that limit the ascent of women by setting "terminal" points for their achievements. According to the authors, no environment is immune from these barriers and consequently, the degree of success for women is limited as they get to the end of their "opportunity rope" much sooner than men. The last two chapters focus on what women can do to advance in the male dominated corporation and what corporations can do to attract the best and the brightest, regardless of gender.

Harel-Giasson, F. "An Analytical Framework for the Training of Women in Management." Paper prepared for the International Conference on Management Training for Women, proceedings of the Workshop on Women, Training and Management, École des hautes études commerciales, August 1987: Montreal, pp. 6-29.

The author asks why so few women are in decision-making positions and why they do not have a greater impact when they are. Five broad categories of responses are proposed — "something" is lacking (training, self-confidence, etc.), the existence of sexual stereotypes, the organization of society which puts women at a disadvantage, the systemic discrimination within organizations and the inability of men and women to work together in an egalitarian situation or when women are in positions of authority. Training is proposed as one of the corrective measures.

Harel-Giasson, F., et Robichaud, J., "Tout savoir sur les femmes cadres d'ici", Actes du colloque tenu à Montréal, les 20 et 21 octobre 1988, Montréal, Les Presses des hautes études commerciales, 1988.

Ce document contient les papiers présentés lors d'un colloque sur la situation actuelle des femmes cadres. Les objectifs du colloque étaient de "faire le point sur la condition présente des femmes cadres d'ici, sur leur apport spécifique à l'entreprise et sur ce que leur réserve l'avenir". On aborde entres autres les sujets suivants — les libertés et les contraintes de faire carrière au féminin, un résumé des éléments historiques, conceptuels et pratiques des femmes gestionnaires depuis 15 ans, un aperçu des femmes cadres de l'avenir au Québec et la conciliation de famille et carrière.

Hébert Germain, G., "Le Syndrome du Bourdon", *L'Actualité*, Avril 1984, p. 43-49.

D'après l'auteur, les hommes ont cessé de réagir aux provocations et stimuli féministes. Au début, parce qu'ils craignaient de ne pas être compris, ensuite, parce qu'ils ont acquis la certitude qu'on ne les écoute pas.

Heilman, M.E., Simon, M.C., and Repper, D.P. "Intentionally Favored, Unitentionally Harmed? Impact of Sex-based Preferential Selection on Self-perceptions and Self-evaluation." *Journal of Applied Psychology*, vol. 72, no. 1, 1987: pp. 62-68.

Using a laboratory setting and male and female undergraduate students, the authors attempted to determine whether there were any differences in the way people reacted to preferential selection as opposed to merit-based selection in playing leadership positions. As anticipated, only women's self-perceptions and self-evaluations were negatively affected by the preferential selection method. Sex-based preferential selection led the women studied to devalue their leadership performance, to take less credit for successful outcomes and less interest in continuing in a leadership role. The authors believe that this research has important implications for the implementation of affirmative action programs. They warn that how such programs are implemented is crucial and they recommend that the focus should be on competence and quality and that those selected should be made aware of this.

Heilman, M.E., and Herlihy, J.M. "Affirmative Action, Negative Reaction? Some Moderating Conditions." *Organizational Behavior and Human Performance*, vol. 33, 1984: pp. 204-213.

Increasing the number of female role models in traditionally male occupations is seen by some as a way of breaking a vicious cycle where occupations that have a small number of women attract few women. The authors argue that HOW women obtain these jobs is crucial and will influence the interest not only women have in these jobs but also the interest of men. The article summarizes a study that was done on male and female college-bound high school students and discusses the implications of the findings for affirmative action programs. The results suggest the importance of explaining the process by which larger numbers of women are placed in occupations that were in the past reserved for men — women and men in this study came to different conclusions when information was not provided to them. Without evidence to the contrary, men assumed a "non-merit-based placement" of women while women assumed that the female occupants had their jobs on the basis of merit.

Heilman, M.E., and Martell, R.F. "Exposure to Successful Women: Antidote to Sex Discrimination in Applicant Screening Decisions?" *Organizational Behavior and Human Decision Processes*, vol. 37, 1986: pp. 376-390.

Increased exposure to successful women is often presented as the solution to occupational bias — as it is known that women can handle traditionally male jobs, the incidence of sex discrimination will decline it is believed and discrimination will disappear. In this research, the authors wanted to determine whether and under what conditions exposure to successful women in non-traditional occupations would mitigate against sex bias in selection decisions. One hundred and forty-six male and female college students participated in this study. The data demonstrate, according to the authors, that exposure to successful women in male dominated occupations can deter subsequent sex discrimination in applicant screening decisions. However, the circumstances under which this is likely to occur are quite limited. Although the situation was simulated, the results suggest that an increase in exposure to successful women in and of itself is not a remedy for sex discrimination.

Heilman, M.E., Martell, R.F., and Simon, M.C. "The Vagaries of Sex Bias: Conditions Regulating the Undervaluation, Equivaluation and Overvaluation of Female Job Applicants." *Organizational Behavior and Human Decision Processes*, vol. 41, 1988: pp. 98-110.

A great number of studies have shown that when women apply for non-traditional jobs, they are evaluated less favourably than men with equivalent qualifications. The authors sought to determine, through this study, the conditions under which women are undervalued, equally valued and overvalued relative to men when they are seeking traditionally male jobs. An experiment was done with 241 college students. The authors found evidence of undervaluation, equivaluation and overvaluation of women relative to men. Unless performance ability was verified (through information on the applicant's abilities) women's ratings only exceeded those given to men when the job in question was perceived to be extremely atypical for a woman.

Henning, M., and Jardin, A. *The Managerial Woman*, New York: Simon and Schuster Pocket Book, 1977.

The major contribution of this book lies in its analysis of the "women who made it" by researching communalities in their upbringing, education, and in the socialization process. It also provides alternatives that are available to both men and women to ensure a woman's career success.

Henning, M., and Jardin, A. *The Managerial Woman*. New York: Anchor Press/Doubleday, 1977.

The book provides an analysis of the differences between men and women managers and patterns in the lives and careers of 25 women in top management positions. The final section suggests what women and men can do to integrate women into management.

Hunt, C. "The Equal Opportunities for Women Program in the Federal Public Service." M.A. Thesis, University of Manitoba, 1987.

This thesis evaluates the Equal Opportunities for Women Program and also examines the implementation of the program from a regional perspective. As well, case studies on four regional offices in Manitoba are included. The author concludes that after twelve years of EOW policy, the opportunities for advancement for women were more limited than they were for men, this in spite of the fact that the implementation of the program coincided with a period of unprecedented increase in the participation of women in the work force. According to the author, no single component can be held responsible for the failure of the program. Rather, a number of factors are cited. Included are a lack of "a single, integrated equal opportunity policy and adequate administrative leadership," little real government commitment, little management accountability for results, systemic barriers in the staffing process, an inflexible "merit" system and societal attitudes.

Huppert-Laufer, J., *La Féminité neutralisée? Les femmes cadres dans l'entreprise*, Paris, Flammarion, 1982.

Suite à une enquête auprès d'une soixantaine de femmes cadres et d'une trentaine de cadres masculins repartis dans treize entreprises, l'auteure revoit l'évolution de la situation des femmes cadres dans l'entreprise. Elle se préoccupe de la question de la conciliation entre une recherche de l'égalité avec les hommes et le maintien de la différence dans un environnement dominé par les hommes, et la réaction des hommes face à une féminisation croissante des postes de cadres. Le dilemme entre vie professionnelle et vie privée apparait comme permanent et le rôle maternel qui est vécu par les femmes cadres apparait comme les plus difficilement conciliable et pour les femmes cadres et pour l'entreprise.

Huppert-Laufer, J., "Les femmes cadres dans l'entreprise: féminité et organisation", *Gestion*, **vol. 9, no. 1, février 1984, p. 46-53.**

Cet article est inspiré du livre *La féminité neutralisée?* du même auteure. Les carrières des femmes cadres sont analysées et l'auteure présente quatre types de "carrière au féminin" — la soumission à la différence, la reconnaissance de la différence, l'exploitation de la différence et la revendication de la différence. C'est l'évolution de ce dernier genre qui modifie ou qui remet en cause l'équilibre des pouvoirs et les structures organisationnelles qui garantissaient la suprématie masculine car cette dernière veut être cadre, épouse ET mère. Quoique l'avenir n'est pas si claire, l'auteure conclut, que, si jusqu'à maintenant la théorie des organisations a été écrite au masculin, il faudrait désormais commencer à comprendre l'entreprise au masculin-féminin.

Hurst, C. "Mathophobia." *Herizons*, **vol. 3, no 1, January-February 1985: pp. 33-34.**

Discusses the notion that women cannot do math. The female stereotype that places heavy emphasis on winning approval from others may have radically altered females' approach to learning.

Johnson, A. "Women Managers: Old Stereotypes Die Hard." *Management Review*, **December 1987: pp. 31-42.**

The author reviews the obstacles female managers face — an "old boy" frame of reference that excludes women, myths about women's goals and abilities, sex-segregated workplaces and absence of long-term goals by women. In order to reduce discrimination against the hiring and promotion of women, employers are advised to "adjust" structurally and attitudinally. Suggestions on how to break down the informal and unstructured barriers that exist both within and outside the organization are included as well as a brief description of progressive efforts by five major American employers in recruiting, retaining and developing female managers.

Kanter, R.S. "Men and Women of the Corporation Revisited." *Management Review*, March 1987: pp. 14-16.

Men and Women of the Corporation, published ten years ago, argued that productivity, motivation and career success for men and women were determined largely by organizational structure and the nature of the social circumstances in which people found themselves. In short, men and women in similar circumstances behaved in similar ways. The problem was, according to Kanter, that women were rarely in similar circumstances because of sex-typed images and their concentration in jobs with lower opportunities for advancement. Although much progress has been made since that time, the author observes that women have not yet penetrated the "glass ceiling" and are kept out of the higher positions. Managerial cloning perpetuates opportunity and power problems. The spread of innovative management practices that could create new opportunities for women will also create new problems, Kanter believes, as long as women carry a disproportionate share of family responsibilities.

Kates, J. "The Quiet Revolution." *Report on Business*, July 1988: pp. 59-64.

This article highlights the progress of women in management in corporate Canada. In spite of this progress, women are still facing barriers, three of which are highlighted here — the difficulty some men (including young men) have working with women, women's own ignorance of team play and the corporate culture that excludes women. The author concludes rather optimistically that the current trend to downsizing could create more hospitable environments for women.

Katz, D. "Sex Discrimination in Hiring: The Influence of Organizational Climate and Need for Approval on Decision Making Behavior." *Psychology of Women Quarterly*, vol. 11, 1987: pp. 11-20.

The author's thesis was that organizational climate could encourage or inhibit discriminatory behaviour and that a person's need for approval would interact with the organization's climate to influence their decisions. Using male business students in a classroom setting, the author states that his thesis received partial support — in a discriminatory climate, female applicants were evaluated less favourably than men in terms of their likelihood of being hired and of being seen as fitting into the organization. However, approval motivation was not related to salary decisions. The finding that organizational climate can have an impact on hiring decisions is important, the author states, because it suggests that environments that encourage non-discriminatory decisions can be consciously created. Variables such as the corporate philosophy, the use of language and the presence of a significant number of women in the management structure can contribute to a non-discriminatory climate.

Keeton, K., *Femme de demain — Un regard lucide et optimiste sur l'avenir des femmes*, Québec, Le Jour, Editeur, 1985.

La quatrième section intitulé "L'activité professionnelle" (chapitres 10, 11 et 12), est d'intérêt particulier. L'auteure mise beaucoup sur les progrès technologiques pour améliorer le sort professionnel des femmes et pour éliminer plusieurs obstacles. Cependant, le fait que peu de filles entrant à l'université s'orientent vers une carrière scientifique l'inquiète beaucoup et des conseils pratiques sont offerts pour tenter de rémédier à la situation. Un avenir plus libre et diversifié pour tous et en particulier les femmes, est anticipé.

Kempeneers, M., "Questions sur les femmes et le travail: une lecture de la crise", *Sociologie et sociétés*, vol. XIX, no. 1, avril 1987, p. 57-71.

Le bouleversement des structures de l'emploi et de la famille depuis les vingt dernières années amènent l'auteure à étudier les trajectoires féminines et les interruptions d'emploi. L'analyse des données invite, selon l'auteure, à reconsidérer l'explication des responsabilités maternelles comme cause principale de la discontinuité en emploi des femmes. Ce sont plutôt, selon l'auteure, des raisons liées aux conditions et à la nature du marché du travail actuel.

Knopf, R. "On Proving Discrimination: Statistical Methods and Unfolding Policy Logics." *Canadian Public Policy*, vol. 12, no. 4, December 1986: pp. 573-583.

The author discusses the use of statistical evidence in the proof of illegal discrimination. Different methods are listed that can be used to prove systemic or intentional discrimination.

Lalande, S., "Les femmes en affaires; une minorité plus que visible", *Le Devoir économique*, mars-avril 1987, p. 26-30.

L'auteure survole le monde des femmes d'affaires, des femmes entrepreneures ou collaboratrices et des femmes cadres. Quoiqu'elles sont présentes de plus en plus à tous les niveaux, la direction des entreprises demeurent toujours un monde masculin. Quatre obstacles sont soulignés: le stéréotype masculin du manager, l'homogénéité au sommet, l'unique modèle de carrière qui rentre souvent en conflit avec l'horloge biologique des femmes et l'absence des femmes dans le réseau informel des clubs sociaux. L'importance des programmes de discrimination positive est aussi soulignée. Plus en plus de femmes choisissent de lancer leur propre entreprise car elles se voient souvent sous-estimées, sous-utilisées et sous-payées dans les grandes entreprises.

Larwood, L., Gutek, B., and Gattiker, U. "Perspectives on Institutional Discrimination and Resistance to Change." *Group and Organization Studies*, vol. 9, no. 3, September 1984: pp. 333-352.

The authors contend that a review of the evidence concerning the efforts to counter discrimination in the workplace suggests that little progress has been made. Three leading theoretical perspectives on discrimination are reviewed — economic, sociological and psychological. However, they are found to be wanting and the authors propose a fourth perspective — the managerial perspective that they call the "rational bias" because it appears that discrimination is the result of a rational decision made in an organizational context. The self-interested manager will not only consider his/her own preferences but also the perceived preferences of relevant powerful others both within or outside the organization. To eliminate discrimination at the organizational level, efforts must be made by the power holders to indicate that discrimination is not acceptable. Some suggestions are included. The authors conclude that although many regulations are currently in place in many organizations, it appears that a commitment by key individuals has been lacking so far.

Larwood, L., Szwajkowski, E., and Rose S. "When Discrimination Makes 'Sense': the Rational Bias Theory." *Women and Work*, ed. Gutek, B.A., Stromberg, A.H., and Larwood, L., vol. 3, 1988: pp. 265-288.

The rational bias theory conceives of discrimination as the consequence of self-interested managers making personnel decisions concerning their subordinates based on the managers' own careers rather than on the abilities of their subordinates. The discrimination has therefore proven difficult to eradicate.

Lasvergnas, I., "Contexte de socialisation primaire et choix d'une carrière scientifique chez les femmes", *Recherches féministes*, 1988, vol. 1, no. 1, p. 31-45.

L'auteure s'attarde sur les facteurs de socialisation des filles en science et constate qu'institutionnellement et relationnellement le support d'une image paternelle dans les institutions scientifiques présente plus de difficulté pour les femmes que pour la plupart des hommes. Selon l'auteure, il existe en science un jeu social construit sur l'homme, où la femme ne s'intègre vraiment jamais.

Laufer, J., "Égalité professionnelle: un atout pour gérer les ressources humaines", *Revue française de gestion*, no. 55, Paris, janvier-février, 1986, p. 41-53.

L'auteur étudie les enjeux de l'adoption d'une loi, introduite en 1983, qui insère dans le code français du travail le droit à l'égalité profession-nelle entre les hommes et les femmes. On souligne que la féminisation croissante de la main d'oeuvre n'a pas réduit la différence entre les emplois occupés par les hommes et par les femmes et que les femmes rencontrent davantage d'obstacles pour obtenir de la formation et une promotion. Les mesures et stratégies préconisées par les plans d'action déposés par les employeurs annuellement sont revues et quoique la nature des entreprises est très diverse, un point commun ressort — la place faite aux femmes — elles sont quasiment absentes des catégories les plus élevées.

Laufer, J., "Les femmes cadres dans l'organisation" dans *Le Sexe du Travail*, par un collectif de femmes, Presses universitaires de Grenoble, 1984, p. 71-95.

Ce texte débute avec un bref historique sur le travail traditionnel des femmes dans les grandes entreprises — un travail généralement de subordonné. En deuxième lieu, l'auteure décrit quatre catégories de femmes cadres. Par la suite elle étudie l'organisation face à la femme cadre qui revendique l'égalité. L'hypothèse de l'auteure est que "...l'intrusion des femmes à des postes de plus en plus semblables à ceux des hommes ... ne peut que renforcer la crise d'identité des hommes et leur désir d'asseoir leur légimité sur ... l'exclusivité de l'adhésion et de l'interprétation correcte des règles".

Laurent A., *Féminin Masculin, le Nouvel Équilibre*, Ed. du Seuil, 1975.

Cet ouvrage montre comment la sortie de la femme du foyer a provoqué certains déséquilibres dans le couple et s'interroge sur les façons dont masculinité et féminité peuvent être conjugués. Pour cela, A. Laurent montre que plus que la femme, c'est l'homme qui pose problème, cet homme agressif et qui tente de conjurer son anxiété par la domination.

Legault, G. et Tardy, E., "Les programmes d'accès à l'égalité au Québec: une condition nécessaire mais non suffisante pour assurer l'égalité des femmes," *Revue de droit*, Université de Sherbrooke, vol. 17, no. 1, 1986, p. 151-189.

Ce texte trace un bref historique des revendications des Québécoises en matière d'égalité en emploi et présente une synthèse des politiques et des programmes mis en place aux Etats-Unis, au Canada et au Québec pour corriger ces inégalités. Selon les auteurs, l'égalité en emploi pour les femmes est une lutte non gagnée et le texte tente de démontrer la sexisation des marchés de travail. En dernier lieu, les enjeux autour des programmes d'accès à l'égalité sont discutés et affirment les auteurs, plus les femmes demandent des mesures correctives, plus l'opposition s'intensifie.

Lewis, G.B. "Progress Toward Racial and Sexual Equality in the Federal Civil Service?" *Public Administration Review*, May/June, 1988: pp. 701-707.

The author notes that the American federal government, as one of the country's largest employers, is a symbol of America's commitment to racial and sexual equality. Its past record has been poor — white males hold most of the high-paying, policy-making jobs. This paper examines the changes between 1976 and 1986 in terms of representativeness and salary differences for five racial and ethnic groups of men and women in the federal civil service. The author concludes that, although women and minorities made progress throughout this period, the pace was slow although steady. At this rate, it would take another 30 years before women and minorities filled half the positions at the GS-13 level (General Schedule white collar pay system).

Lisée, J.F., "L'entreprise des mères", *Revue Commerce*, mai 1988, p. 114-118.

L'auteur présente une perspective québecoise sur la situation des femmes aux États-Unis. Les entreprises américaines s'empressent de répondre aux besoins spécifiques des femmes seulement lorsqu'elles s'aperçoivent que les femmes sont devenues indispensables dans le marché du travail. Les mécanismes utilisés incluent garderies, horaires flexibles, congés de maternité, modification des critères de promotion (plutôt que de considérer les années de travail consécutives, on additionne toutes les années de travail sans regard aux interruptions), travail à la maison, accès à un congé de maladie quand l'enfant est malade, etc... Cependant, ces précédents sont souvent seulement établis pour celles rendues indispensables par leur compétence. Les entreprises dirigées par les femmes sont apparamment plus conscientes des problèmes de leurs employés et modifient leurs pratiques en conséquence. Selon l'auteur, dans un marché du travail en voie de retrécissement, des conditions de travail plus favorables à la maternité et à la famille, peuvent devenir un avantage pour l'employeur.

Loden, M. "Recognizing Women's Potential: No Longer Business as Usual." *Management Review*, December 1987: pp. 44-46.

The author identifies ten strategies that can help employees create an organizational climate that fully uses women's talents and skills. Comprehensive efforts in the areas of recruitment, development and retention are required. Some of the recommended initiatives include rectifying inequities in salaries and promotions, creating executive women's councils reporting to the CEO, tracking high-potential women, emphasizing commitment through communication, encouraging networking, updating policies and benefit plans to better reflect changing times, and providing education and awareness training.

Lord, C., "Programmes d'accès à l'égalité: où en est le dossier?", *La Gazette des femmes*, mai-juin, 1987, p. 14-17.

L'auteure résume les grandes lignes du programme d'accès à l'égalité (programme inclus dans la partie III de la charte québecoise des droits et libertés de la personne) — les entreprises touchées, le soutien financier et technique disponible et l'existence d'un comité consultatif. L'expérience d'Hydro-Québec est résumée. A souligner qu'à Hydro-Québec un projet pilote a intégré des femmes dans un milieu non-traditionnel, non pas d'une façon isolée, mais six par six. Les avantages d'ouvrir les portes des entreprises publiques et parapubliques aux femmes sont aussi soulignées.

Lowe, G.S. *Women in the Administrative Revolution*. Toronto: University of Toronto Press, 1987.

The causes and consequences of the feminization of clerical work in Canada with some comparative analysis with Great Britain is the subject of this book. Chapter 4 presents an in-depth look at the conditions under which clerical work became feminized using the banking sector and the federal civil service as case studies. Referring to women working in the federal service as "third division civil servants," the author notes that the early discriminatory policies of the federal civil service were so successful that their effects still impact on today's employment structure. Noting the cumulative effect of sex labelling and job segregation, the author contends that once sex-typing of an occupation has occurred, a kind of structural inertia sets in and it is difficult to break the pattern. As well, the working conditions of the "female" jobs lead to a certain adaptation by women — low job commitment, higher turnover, etc., which reinforces the image of women as only suitable for these kinds of jobs.

Mann, A. "Women Managers: Destroying the Myths." *Management Today*, March 1987: pp. 66-67.

Women managers are striving to gain more senior jobs in management. The article points out how firms can accommodate the special needs of women better, to the advantage of both parties.

Marchis-Mousen, M.F. Women in Management Worldwide — *A Research Review*. **Montreal: École des hautes études commerciales, January 1989.**

This paper presents a review and a good summary of the findings on women in management throughout the world. After providing a brief overview of the current overall situation of women managers, the author identifies three types of barriers they face — socio-cultural barriers such as socialization and stereotypes and the repercussions that these two variables have had on the way women managers are evaluated and perceived; situational barriers within organizations, both social and structural, including policies and procedures, internal labour markets, sex ratios, etc. and lastly, family commitments. Another section deals with the key attributes of success and mentoring is highlighted as one such element. Lastly, three types of corrective measures to the barriers women managers face — legislation, organizational change and training — are summarized.

Markham, W.T. "Sex, Relocation and Occupational Advancement: The 'real cruncher' for Women." *Women and Work: An Annual Review*, vol. 2, 1987: pp. 207-231.

An analysis of the effects of relocation on the careers of women and men is presented through a review of the literature on the relationships between sex, geographic mobility and job advancement. The evidence suggests that relocation enhances the career of those who move for their own advancement, that women move less often to advance their careers and are less willing to do so. The evidence regarding why this is so is presently not adequate according to the author and further study is required.

Markiewicz, D., and Devine, I. "Cross-Sex Relationships at Work and the Impact of Gender Stereotypes." Paper presented at the Women in Management Symposium, Mount Saint Vincent University, Nova Scotia, 1988, pp. 3.1-3.9.

This study measures the effects of sex on judgments of performance, of affective variables, of consequences for careers and of fellow workers' reactions. It shows that specific circumstances are associated with particular patterns of responses.

Marshall, J. *Women Managers — Travellers in a Male World.* Chichester: John Wiley and Sons, 1984.

The author argues that society and the world of organizations are largely structured by men and dominated by their needs and values. "Think manager, think male" is still widely accepted and women are acceptable in management if their behaviour and career patterns are the same as men's. The author reviews in some depth the current literature on the management potential of women and looks at the obstacles (with particular emphasis on the informal structures) that keep women from advancing and that hinder them when they move into more senior positions. Several chapters are devoted to a research study of 30 British female managers and leads the author to con-clude that the notions of career and ambition need to be revised when studying women. One chapter maps out advice to organizations on how to get more women into management. Proposed initiatives include integrating women as equals (number balancing, training, etc.), improving the acceptance of women and advising women on how to participate in a man's world. However, the author maintains that this strategy has limited value in the long term and proposes more radical solutions emphasizing women and their experiences rather than men's.

Marshall, J. "A Testing Time Full of Potential." *Women in Management Review*, vol. 1, no. 1, spring 1985: pp. 5-14.

The author believes that we are "at the start of a new stage in women's development" and that this will impact on women in management. Four trends are discussed — the movement away from male models of management to diverse models, the creation of "women-only spares," the increasing identification and support among women and the importance of developing opportunities for dialogue between men and women.

Marshall, K., "Présence accrue des femmes dans les professions, depuis le début des années 80", *Tendances sociales canadiennes,* **Statistique Canada, printemps 1989, p. 13-16.**

Les statistiques de 1986 indiquent que les femmes ont fait des progrès rapides dans les professions à prédominance masculine. Mais, en dépit des gains réalisés, les femmes continuent d'être fortement sous-représentés dans la plupart des professions à prédominance masculine. L'auteure souligne aussi des différences quant aux caractéristiques d'emploi des hommes et des femmes dans les professions — les femmes sont toujours moins bien rémunérées que les hommes et cet écart n'a pas diminué depuis 1981.

Martin, P., Harrison, D., and Dinitto, D. "Advancement for Women in Hierarchical Organizations: A Multilevel Analysis of Problems and Prospects." *The Journal of Applied Behavioral Science,* **vol. 19, no. 1, 1983: pp. 19-33.**

Women's problems and prospects for advancement to upper-level positions in hierarchical organizations are analyzed within a five-level framework of social organization. The five levels are (1) societal; (2) institutional; (3) organizational; (4) role; and (5) invidivual. Corresponding units of analysis for each level are identified and discussed. To illustrate the framework, two problems confronting women are identified for each level, along with possible corrective actions. Conclusions are that (1) fundamental change in women's status in hierarchical work organizations will require simultaneous efforts on all five levels of social organization; (2) change in any realm requires political actions against ideological justificant and claims for women's exclusion; and (3) the division of labour between the sexes in relation to work and child/family/home responsibilities must change before women can receive equitable treatment in the workplace. The authors call for more research on the interrelations between influence and factors across levels of social organization.

Maruani, M., *Mais Qui a Peur du Travail des Femmes?,* **Paris, Editions Syros, 1985.**

L'auteure fait le point sur la transformation radicale depuis vingt ans du travail des femmes hors de la famille en France. Mais en dépit des faits et des lois et en dépit de l'expansion de l'emploi féminin, "le droit à l'emploi des femmes n'est toujours pas acquis" selon l'auteure. Cette croissance ne s'est pas accompagnée d'une plus grande "mixité" des emplois et celles qui s'aventurent dans les occupations traditionnellement masculines font souvent face au phénomène d'exclusion et voient souvent une division sexuelle du travail se recréer. La réalité du travail pour les femmes est niée, estime l'auteure, parce que ça fait peur — et ça fait peur parce que ça touche aux rapports de pouvoir et d'autorité entre hommes et femmes.

McCaney, M., Ahmed, S. et al. "The Subjective Culture of Public Sector Women and Men Managers: A Common Instrumental/ Expressive Value Orientation or, Two Different Worlds?" *Canadian Journal of Administrative Sciences*, **vol. 6, no. 2, June 1989: pp. 54-63.**

This study was designed to determine if there would be any difference in the meanings of work values for male and female managers. The subjects were male and female managers in the federal public service. No significant differences across gender were found and the authors discuss the implications of this study for employment equity.

McEnrue, M.P. "Predicting Attitudes Toward Affirmative Action in Advancement." *Equal Opportunities International (UK)*, **vol. 7, no. 1, 1988: pp. 28-31.**

Demographic changes, pending court decisions, and corporate downsizing have caused the press to place more emphasis on affirmative action in advancement as opposed to initial selection. Some research suggests that women and minorities have turned down advancement opportunities when they exist, and a number of explanations have been proposed as to why they voluntarily refuse to pursue these promotion opportunities. A study investigates such refusal based on the perception that the promotion opportunities are really phantom. It also considers the impact of this phenomenon on workers' attitudes toward affirmative action. Eighty female and minority employees involved in low-level administrative and high-level technical or clerical positions at a university participated in the research. Results indicate that a link exists between employees' advancement aspirations, perceptions of opportunity, and their attitudes concerning affirmative action. Tables. Charts. References.

McNeish, J. *Study of the Differentiated Career Orientation Between Men and Women.* **Research paper, Concordia University, April 1980.**

This study attempted to correlate career anchorage with certain independent variables of organizational behaviour. Findings emphasize that no difference could be found between men and women in terms of need for achievement, locus of control, age, participation in decision-making, job scope, motivation and organizational independence.

McPherson, J.A. "Mobilizing the Mentor." *The Entrepreneurship Development Review*, **no. 4, winter 1978: pp. 18-19.**

This paper discusses two alternate approaches to assisting new entrepreneurs to access the resources they need to plan, launch and manage a new enterprise. Community-based advisors of start-up entrepreneurs are encouraged to adopt a networking approach rather than a hands-on mentoring technique, as a more efficient and effective counselling methodology.

Merriam, S. "Mentors and Proteges: A Critical Review of the Literature." *Adult Education Quarterly*, **vol. 33, no. 3, 1983: pp. 161-173.**

Within the last few years, mentoring has emerged as a popular topic in several fields. Articles and talk shows imply that success in life is somehow related to having a mentor or being a mentor. The purpose of this review is to evaluate the extent to which such enthusiasm can be substantiated by research. The literature on mentoring is divided into three sections: the mentoring phenomenon in adult growth and development, mentoring in the business world, and mentoring in academic settings. A concluding section summarizes findings across these three settings, speculates about the relevance of mentoring for adult educators, and suggests avenues for future inquiry.

Metcalfe, B.P. "What Motivates Managers: An Investigation by Gender and Sector of Employment." *Public Administration*, **vol. 67, spring 1989: pp. 95-108.**

This study presents the findings of a large survey of attitudes of British managers to what they want from their jobs and how they see their jobs meeting those needs. Men and women managers from both the private and public sectors were included. The author concludes that there appears to be little foundation to the myth that women are less ambitious and career-oriented than men. The data also suggest that in both the public and private sectors, women have to make decisons re: marriage and children that men do not appear to have to make.

Meynaud, H.Y., "L'accès au dernier cercle — A propos de la participation des femmes aux instances de pouvoir dans les entreprises", *Revue française des affaires sociales,* **42ᵉ année, no. 1, jan.-mars 1988, p. 67-87.**

La première partie de ce travail décrit certains des blocages que les femmes rencontrent dans leur tentative de monter l'échelle du pouvoir. La deuxième section présente les points de vue des femmes en étudiant particulièrement leur trajectoire de carrière. Tout comme en Amérique, l'auteure souligne l'absence des femmes dans le "dernier cercle" et note qu'à "diplôme égale, ancienneté égale" la carrière des femmes est plus lente. Les obstacles sont aussi semblables à ceux qu'on retrouve en Amérique — la résistance des décideurs (souvent à cause de mythes et stéréotypes au sujet des femmes), des barrages systématiques, certains obstacles d'ordre légal et des hésitations par les femmes elles-mêmes. Quelques exemples d'un début de changement sont notés, y inclus l'importance de la mise en application de lois sur l'égalité professionnelle des femmes. Mais l'auteure avertit que l'insertion des femmes sans précautions préalables peut aussi conduire à l'échec.

Mikalachki, D., and Mikalachki, A. "Women in Business — Going for Broke," *Business Quarterly,* **vol. 50, no. 2, 1985: pp. 25-32.**

The authors review the status of professional and managerial women in Canada between 1975 and the early 1980s and present the results of a study of MBA women and men undertaken by them in 1984 and 1985. The results showed differences between the two groups in terms of the importance of their careers, the level of management attained, their career goals and the obstacles they saw with regard to their career growth. Attitudes towards their gender, family responsibilities and geographical limitations were identified by women but not by male managers as barriers to their career growth.

Miller, J., Lincoln, J.R., and Olson, J. "Relationality and Equity in Professional Networks: Gender and Race as Factors in the Stratification of Inter-organizational Systems." *American Journal of Sociology*, vol. 87, 1981: pp. 308-335.

The organizational principles of rationality and equity account for the bureaucratic leveling effect on social differences posited by Weber. An inference from this framework, that organizational systems will neither create nor reinforce inequality based on gender or race, was examined with data provided by the members of six multi-agency social service delivery systems. The dependent variable was a measure of access to the networks of inter-organizational exchange that tied together the agencies in these systems. This measure, called centrality, did not vary by race or gender. However, an analysis of first- and second-order interaction effects indicated that the combinations of investments and contributions that were predictive of men, and non-white women. A complicated process of negotiation for resources and advantages was indicated that is not easily reconciled with deductions from classical organizational theory.

Ministère des Affaires Municipales, Gouvernement de l'Ontario, *Tendances de l'Emploi dans les Administrations Municipales Selon le Sexe — Initiatives et Evolution,* **décembre 1986.**

Cette étude descriptive fournit des renseignements sur la place des femmes dans le secteur des administrations municipales. La gamme des emplois pour les femmes est plus restreinte que celle des hommes et dans les secteurs où travaillent la majorité des femmes, l'échelle des salaires est inférieure à celle des hommes. Il ressort aussi de cette analyse que "plus la municipalité est grande, plus le pourcentage des postes administratifs occupés par les femmes est faible".

Moore, L.L., ed., *Not As Far As You Think.* **Massachusetts: Lexington Books, 1986.**

The internal-psychological barriers and the external barriers women face at work are discussed and some solutions are offered. Of particular interest are two chapters on managing the culture of an organization (Chapter 4, Mentoring or Networking by R. Keele and Chapter 12, Mastering Change: The Skills We Need by R.M. Kanter). According to the author, the problems are both internal and external and therefore call for individual male and female changes as well as institutional and organizational changes.

Morazain, J., "La difficile ascension des femmes dans l'entreprise", *Le magazine Affaires*, **septembre 1985, p. 19-31.**

Malgré une progression remarquable depuis la dernière décennie, les femmes cadres sont presque toujours absentes des postes décisionnels. La recherche démontre, selon l'auteure, que plus on monte, plus il y a des tendances à l'homogénéité car les critères de compétence sont plus flous et les décideurs vont chercher ceux qu'ils connaissent, ceux avec qui ils ont une affinité. L'auteure se penche sur la situation des femmes cadres et note les obstacles systématiques qu'elles rencontrent — leur absence dans les réseaux masculins, l'absence de modèles féminins de progression, l'absence de mentors, et les préjugés persistants qu'elles doivent subir (la discrimination subtile, l'inconfort des hommes face à leurs collègues féminins, les présomptions; face à la mobilité, la disponibilité et l'ambition des femmes mariées). Les handicaps psychologiques des femmes sont aussi notés tels que leur incapacité de déléguer au niveau familial, leur manque de confiance et leur manque de visibilité. L'importance d'une stratégie de carrière est soulignée. Quatre entrevues avec des femmes cadres font suite. Elles offrent des conseils pratiques au niveau de l'individu tels l'importance du sens de l'équipe, d'avoir des objectifs, la formation et la nécessité de programme d'accès à l'égalité.

Morazain, J., "L'égalité des chances — entre l'essentiel et le superflu", *Le magazine Affaires*, **octobre 1985, p. 21.**

Cet article porte sur la nécessité d'un coup de pouce pour contrecarrer les obstacles à l'entrée et à la progression des femmes sur le marché du travail. Le débat s'accentue cependant quand vient le temps d'identifier les moyens les plus appropriés — doit-on forcer les employeurs ou laisser jouer librement les tendances du marché? L'auteure retrace l'historique de ces programmes et des actions du gouvernement fédéral et du gouvernement du Québec et remet le défi aux employeurs de démontrer que les mesures règlementaires ne sont pas nécessaires pour remédier aux situations d'inégalités courantes.

Moreira, P. "Myths About Women Hinder Advancement." Halifax Chronicle Heral, June 7, 1988: pp. 1-B & 2-B.

The article reviews some of the myths about women in the workplace. The author then goes on to explore employment equity plans and the important elements that these should reflect.

Morgan, N. *Implosion: An Analysis of the Growth of the Federal Public Service in Canada (1945-1985)*. Montreal: The Institute for Research on Public Policy, 1986.

Analyzes the growth of the federal public service over a forty-year period. The author contends that the growth was not managed and has led to an "unbalanced" work force that is characterized by too many male middle managers concentrated in the Ottawa-Hull region. Women were the "biggest losers" according to the author in both periods of public service expansion that she reviews. This is attributed to a lack of political will on the part of two prime ministers (contrary to their position on bilingualism and the hiring of Francophones). Morgan also maintains that during the last expansion, the evaluation and merit systems were allowed to break down. She speculates briefly on the future of the public service.

Morgan, N., *Jouer à l'inégalité: Les femmes et la fonction publique fédérale du Canada (1908-1987)*, Ottawa, Conseil consultatif canadien de la situation de la femme, 1988.

L'auteure fait l'historique de la progression des femmes au sein de la Fonction publique fédérale et fait état des barrières formelles et informelles qui ont empêché et retardé leur recrutement et leur promotion. Les écarts entre les hommes et les femmes sont toujours existants et ceci en dépit de programmes spéciaux, d'un recrutement plus féminin et d'un taux de promotion pour les femmes qui est, depuis quelques temps supérieur à celui des hommes. Sa thèse principale est "l'extraordinaire résistance" des hommes au partage du territoire bureaucratique, leur utilisation du système informel pour ériger des barrières techniques à la progression des femmes et l'absence d'unité ou de solidarité chez les femmes. Sa recherche est basée sur l'histoire de la fonction publique à partir d'archives, de rapports annuels, de statistiques fournies par la Commission de la fonction publique et d'entrevues ouvertes avec cinquante-deux fonctionnaires.

Morrison, A.M., et al, and the Centre for Creative Leadership, *Breaking the Glass Ceiling: Can Women Reach the Top of America's Largest Corporations*. Reading, Mass.: Addison-Wesley Publishing Company, 1987.

Based on a three-year study of 76 women in or near the management level at 25 Fortune 100-sized companies and on a companion study with 22 "savvy insiders," the authors examined the factors that determined success or derailment for women in the corporate world. Central to their thesis is that not only is there a glass ceiling, a "transparent barrier" that keeps women (because they are women) from rising above a certain level in corporations, but once women break this barrier, they meet a wall — a "wall of tradition and stereotype" that keeps them out of the inner circle of senior management or the club. The authors are not optimistic about women's chances of entering the senior management level over the next 20 years. Changes in institutions, in attitudes and in behaviour are required. Some mechanisms that individual companies have used to reduce barriers are identified and the enforcement of formal legislation such as the *Equal Employment Opportunity Act* is recommended.

Morrison, A., White, P.R., and Van Velson, E. "Executive Women: Substance Plus Style." *Psychology Today*, August 1987: pp. 18-26.

The authors describe the "narrow band" of acceptable behaviour for women executives and identify four contradictory sets of expectations that women must reconcile: taking risks, but being consistently outstanding; being tough, but not too tough; being ambitious but not expecting equal treatment particularly in the areas of salary, budgets and access to benefits; and taking responsibility but following other's advice. Mounting evidence indicates, the authors point out, that women are "remarkably similar" to men in their abilities and motives. However, women in management have been perceived as more different from men than they really are and this has led to a qualitatively different environment for women from the one executive men operate in. The authors believe that this difference may be the "crucial" and perhaps the only meaningful difference between male and female executives.

Morrow, J. "Employment Equity Planning." *Canadian Public Administration*, vol. 29, no. 4, 1986: pp. 630-632.

The author underlines the need for employment equity planning in the public sector and highlights some of the elements that can help make it an important management tool. A strong executive commitment to the principles, implementation strategy and outcomes of the program is seen as crucial. An educational strategy, as opposed to a coercive strategy, is proposed and it is recommended that the program be linked to a human resource and career development strategy. The author concludes by identifying the elements that should be common to employment equity programs regardless of the chosen implementation strategy.

Nelson, D.L., and Quick, J.C. "Professional Women: Are Distress and Disease Inevitable?" *Academy of Management Review*, **vol. 10, no. 2, 1985: pp. 206-218.**

The authors examined the literature on women to determine the unique stressors affecting professional women. In addition to common stress, which individuals in organizations must contend with, women face unique obstacles that include discrimination (and the more subtle form found in exclusion from the informal systems within organizations), sex-role stereotyping, conflicting demands of career and family life and social isolation. The behavioural, physiological and psychological consequences of distress are reviewed and four preventive "stress management moderators" are suggested. One of these includes finding a mentor. Additional areas of study are also identified.

Nichols, J. *Men's Liberation: A New Definition of Masculinity.* **New York: Penguin Books, 1975.**

This book proposes a new definition of masculinity. "Men's liberation" means freedom from the destructive competition, from the nervousness that inhibits male friendship, from all the cultural straitjackets and mental stereotypes that alienate men's attitudes and behaviours.

Nicholson, N., and West, M. *Managerial Job Change: Men and Women in Transition.* **Cambridge: Cambridge University Press, 1988.**

The authors are concerned about change and how middle to senior managers experience job change and transitions. The literature on careers, occupational socialization and organizational change is deficient in its attention to the dynamics of adjustment to change, the authors contend. A sample of 2,300 British managers (including 800 women) drawn from a wide range of regions and organization types is the basis of this study. Among the conclusions reached by the authors is the notion of different career paths for men and women. Women in their sample moved faster between jobs and made more radical switches, typically employer-changing and they maintained this pattern more continuously throughout their careers. As well, they had different motives and attitudes to their careers — women had high growth needs and were more intrinsically motivated in career choices. Given the pace of change the traditional notion of "career" is being eroded. The authors argue that the style and pattern of response of women could be more in keeping with the climate of current times than men's.

Nixon, M. "Few Women in School Administration: Some Explanations." *The Journal of Educational Thought*, vol. 21, no. 2, August 1987: pp. 63-70.

The author considers explanations for the small number of women administrators in Canada where, in teaching, there are no structural barriers to upward mobility. Reviewing briefly traditional approaches to this question, the author finds a more plausible explanation in the linking of three dimensions to the model of covert discrimination — role discrimination, access discrimination and treatment discrimination. The problem of the small number of women administrators is, according to the article, symptomatic of a larger problem, that is, the androcentrism (the elevation of the masculine to the level of the universal) that is a part of administrative roles.

Noe, R.A. "Women and Mentoring: A Review and Research Agenda." *Academy of Management Review*, vol. 13, no. 1, 1988: pp. 65-78.

An overview of the research on mentoring is provided. Evidence to date indicates that career and psychosocial benefits do result from mentoring relationships, however, it would appear that women may have difficulty in establishing such relationships. Female mentors are often lacking and the development of cross-gender mentorships can be inhibited by a number of individual or organizational factors such as a lack of access by women to potential mentors, women's status as "tokens" which gives them high visibility in an organization and which can scare off possible mentors, sex-role stereotypes about women managers that make them less desirable as proteges, and peer perceptions that the cross-gender relationships are sexual in nature. It would appear that the lack of mentorships for females can have adverse consequences for both the individual and the organization. The author concludes by highlighting areas for further research.

Northcott, H.C., and Lowe, G.S. "Job & Gender Influences in the Subjective Experience of Work." *Canadian Review of Sociology and Anthropology*, **vol. 24, no. 1, February 1987: pp. 117-131.**

A study of the letter-sorting machine operators and letter carriers at Canada Post was carried out to determine whether males and females react differently to working conditions because of (1) different perspectives (gender) or (2) working conditions, per se. The results support the proposition that working conditions and not gender determine perceptions and reactions to work.

O'Leary, V.E. "Women's Relationships with Women in the Workplace." in *Women and Work*, **vol. 3.**

In an attempt to review the social psychological literature, this article discusses the perception of women in the workplace, as bosses and subordinates, and tries to explain the complex differences between male and female perceptions.

Paquerot, S., "Les Femmes Cadres dans la Fonction Publique du Québec", dans "Tout savoir sur les femmes cadres d'ici", Actes du colloque tenu à Montréal, les 20 et 21 octobre 1988, Montréal, Le Groupe Femmes, Gestion et Entreprises, Les Presses des hautes études commerciales, 1988, p. 243-256.

La place des femmes dans les structures décisionnelles de la fonction publique québécoise est analysée. L'étude tente de démontrer qu'en dépit de la reconnaissance du principe d'égalité d'accès aux postes de pouvoir, la participation aux décisions est toujours hors de la portée des femmes.

Paquette, , L., *La Situation Socio-Economique des Femmes, Faits et Chiffres*, réalisée par le Secrétariat à la condition féminine, Québec, Les Publications du Québec, 1989.

Ce document présente plusieurs séries d'indicateurs statistiques sur la situation socio-économique des Québécoises. Ces indicateurs sont en grande majorité reliés au marché du travail — participation au marché du travail, la formation, les emplois occupés, le travail à temps partiel, etc... Malgré la participation toujours croissante des femmes sur le marché du travail et malgré une scolarisation accrue, la ségrégation professionnelle et les écarts salariaux entre hommes et femmes persistent toujours.

Paton, A. *Women in Management: Affirmative Action and Merit in the Federal Public Service.* Masters Research Project, School of Public Administration, Queen's University, 1985.

The author discusses whether affirmative action or equal opportunity programs are in conflict with the merit principle. She argues that the "objective" merit principle has produced a rather homogeneous civil service and she makes the distinction between the merit principle and the merit system. She states that in fact the notion of "merit" is an evolving one. Better access for women to in-house training and other "non-competitive" benefits that have been denied to them in the past should increase women's chances for promotion. This should also contribute to a more "representative" bureaucracy.

Paul, N. "Networking: Women's Key to Success." *Women in Management Review*, vol. 1, no. 3, 1985: pp. 146-151.

Two obstacles that women in management experience are isolation and loneliness. Networking is one way of overcoming these obstacles according to the author and a guide to networking is provided. The different types of networks, how they are structured, what they are and are not and how they work are included.

Pazy, A. "Sex Differences in Responsiveness to Organizational Career Management." *Human Resource Management*, vol. 26, no. 2, 1987: pp. 243-256.

This is a study of the differences between women and men in their responsiveness to formal organizational career management. It was found that the individual career variables of women were similar to men's, but their responsiveness to organizational career management was higher than men's.

Peck, T. "When Women Evaluate Women, Nothing Succeeds Like Success: The Differential Effects of Status Upon Evaluations of Male and Female Professional Ability." *Sex Roles*, **vol. 4, no. 2, 1978.**

Male and female subjects evaluated articles supposedly written by either a male or a female author of high or low professional status. Although evaluations by the male subjects appeared to be only slightly affected by the status variable, female subjects exhibited a complex reaction to the status variable and gave their most favourable evaluations to the high status woman and their least favourable evaluations to the low status woman. An evaluation-attribution hypothesis is presented to explain this response pattern. The significance of this response pattern for women who are attempting professional success and for the perception of female professional role models is discussed.

Peder, M., and Fritchie, R. "Training Men to Work With Women." *Women in Management Review*, **vol. 1, no. 2, 1985: pp. 75-84.**

The authors maintain that current approaches to improving the number and quality of women managers concentrate in defining and analyzing the barriers to women's mobility and designing positive action programs. However, they miss a crucial point and fail to deal with the "heart of the problem", i.e., people's feelings, values and attitudes. Until this is addressed, the authors maintain that real or lasting change is unlikely.

Peitchinis, S. *Women at Work: Discrimination and Response.* **Toronto: McClelland and Stewart Inc., 1989.**

Women have made important gains in the workplace over the past decade according to the author and "occupational discrimination" has largely disappeared but "employment discrimination" (being hired for suitable work and offered reasonable opportunities for advancement) is still a serious problem. Today's barriers are subtle but "highly effective." Discrimination occurs in the "selection, interviewing (and) hiring process, in the assignment of work responsibilities, in promotions and in pay." This book examines many issues related to women and paid employment. Of particular relevance here are sections dealing with the myths about women that provide the basis and the explanations for discriminatory practices and the occupational distribution of women and why it differs from that of men. The author anticipates that the progress of women into high-level jobs will be slow. The challenge will be to find ways to reduce the subjectivity and arbitrariness of promotions and work assignments with "rules, regulations and procedures" in order that women in both the private and public sectors can attain levels beyond middle management.

Piche, L. "Employment Equity: Managing in a Rights-seeking Environment." *Canadian Public Administration*, vol. 29., no. 4, 1986: pp. 624-630.

The author is concerned with change in an organizational environment and more specifically with the management of change at Canadian National, a Crown corporation with an overwhelmingly male, unionized and blue-collar work force. In order to implement an employment equity program, an analysis of the external environment (such as the state of the economy and industry-specific concerns such as downsizing) was done and internal factors such as the lines of accountability, financial and other resources and the personalities involved were also reviewed. Communications, both within and outside the corporation, was seen to be a very important component of the implementation strategy. As well, employment equity co-ordinators were an integral part of the process. Both short-term and long-term targets were established and some *ad hoc* measures were also used to employ and promote women. The author is of the opinion that there are "signs of a turnaround in credibility" but that progress is "fragile and uneven."

Powell, G.N. *Women and Men in Management*, Newbury Park, California: Sage Publications, 1988.

The author covers a very wide range of topics addressing preorganization and organizational entry issues (childhood socialization, individual career choices, recruitment) as well as individual and organizational issues that arise in the workplace. Gender stereotyping, a major barrier for both men and women, is discussed at length (see particularly Chapters 4 and 5) and the author explores in some depth the research evidence regarding sex differences in managerial behaviour, commitment, motivation and stress. The author also looks at factors that promote or prevent gender stereotyping of peers and notes particularly the impact of the sex ratios or work groups. The evidence, according to the author does not support the traditional belief that men make better managers and concludes that androgynous managers are more effective. Sex differences in career paths are also examined. Each chapter concludes with implications for management including recommended action for change for both organizations and individuals. Also included are recommendations regarding how organizations can best promote equal opportunity within their organizations.

Prévost, N. et al. *Les femmes sur le chemin du pouvoir*, Québec, Conseil du statut de la femme, 1988.

Une recherche statistique qui se veut pûrement descriptive et qui fait état de la situation des femmes au Québec dans les "postes de pouvoir" aux niveaux politique, gouvernemental, économique et éducatif. Les postes électifs et les postes de gestion sont inclus. Le deuxième chapitre porte sur la fonction publique québécoise. L'auteure observe que les femmes sont encore peu nombreuses dans la haute direction de la fonction publique et quoiqu'elles commencent à occuper des emplois supérieurs dans les organismes à vocation sociale et culturelle, elles sont presque totalement absentes des ministères à vocation économique.

Ragins, B.R. "Barriers to Mentoring: The Female Manager's Dilemma." *Human Relations*, vol. 42, no. 1, 1989: pp. 1-22.

Current American research would indicate that female managers are less likely to advance as far or as fast in organizations as their male counterparts. Mentoring relationships or lack thereof for women could be a factor. The author reviews current literature on the interpersonal and organizational barriers female managers encounter in their attempts to develop and maintain "effective" mentoring relationships in organizations. Guidelines for future research are suggested and advice to organizations seeking to address this problem are presented.

***Rapport annuel de la Commission canadienne des droits de la personne*, Ottawa, Ministère des Approvisionnements et Services Canada, 1989.**

Dans son rapport annuel (1988), la Commission déclarait que selon elle "La discrimination fondée sur le sexe est la forme de discrimination la plus répandue et la plus tenace dans notre société..." Le rapport fait état des résultats de la *Loi sur l'équité en matière d'emploi* — les femmes et trois autres groupes défavorisés sont toujours sous-représentés. Même au gouvernement fédéral, lui-même soumis à une politique d'équité en matière d'emploi depuis plusieurs années, la Commission souligne qu'il y a un écart "important" entre le nombre de femmes profession-nelles dans la fonction publique et leur taux de disponibilité à l'échelle nationale. Selon la Commission, il s'agit de modifier des attitudes "profondément ancrées" et d'entamer des "transformations d'ordre systémique". En annexe, on peut retrouver des modifications recom-mandées par la Commission relatives à l'élargissement de la portée de la *Loi sur les droits de la personne* y inclus les programmes d'équité.

Raynolds, E.H. "Management Women in the Corporate Workplace: Possibilities for the Year 2000." *Human Resource Management*, vol. 26, no. 2, 1987: pp. 265-276.

This article considers what corporations' attitudes toward women will be in the year 2000, and what women's attitudes toward corporations will be at that time. Women's current position in the work force is char-acterized. Consideration is given to the direction today's workplace is taking as it makes the transition to the start of a new century. Based on current observations and trends, the article explores the needs and desires of the twenty-first century woman. Four major tools available to corporations preparing to enter the next century are discussed, including family issues, a commitment to innovation, training and women's contributions to the management of transition.

Reif, W.E., Newstrom, J.W., and Monczka, R.M. "Exploding Some Myths About Women Managers." *California Management Review*, vol. 17, no. 4, 1975: pp. 72-79.

Reviews research on the question of whether women managers are psychologically and socially different from men managers. Provides the results of a study that examined whether women's views of formal and informal organizational concepts differ from men's.

Reskin, B., and Hartmann, H. *Women's Work, Men's Work — Sex Segregation on the Job.* Washington: National Academy Press, 1986.

This report prepared by the Committee on Women's Employment and Related Issues reviews evidence of sex segregation and its negative con-sequences for women and for society. It also attempts to explain why women are concentrated in small numbers of less well paying jobs and what can be done to improve women's occupational opportunities.

Two chapters are of particular interest: Chapter 3, "Explaining Sex Segregation in the Workplace" and Chapter 4, "Reducing Sex Segregation in the Workplace." According to the authors, factors that help to account for the sex segregation of work include the cultural beliefs society has about gender and work, barriers to employment, socialization and education, family responsibilities and the occupational opportunity structure. Senior level commitment to equal opportunity is one of many factors identified as being crucial for increasing women's opportunities. Recommendations for further action concentrate on improving the enforcement of equal opportunity laws and expanding efforts in employment and education.

Rosen, B., and Jerdee, T.J. "Sex Stereotyping in the Executive Suite." *Harvard Business Review*, **vol. 52, March-April 1974: pp. 45-58.**

The review surveyed 1,400 subscribers in management positions to determine the extent of unintended sex bias in decision making. The findings indicated greater organizational concern and support for male employees, and the authors concluded that, in matters of career demands and family obligations, personal conduct and selection, promotion and career-development decisions, managers are biased in favour of males.

Rothwell, S. "Cost-effective Approaches to Women's Career Development." *Women in Management Review*, **vol. 1, no. 1, 1985: pp. 30-39.**

Positive action for women is clearly needed the author contends, to increase women's mobility in organizations. However, like all policy proposals, such proposed action must be "cost-effective" and like all change, strategies must be carefully planned. The article describes the strategic planning process required in order to achieve both cost effectiveness and realizing women's potential in the organization.

Rowney, J.I.A., Cahoon, A.R. "Individual and Organizational Characteristics of Women in Managerial Leadership Roles." *Women in Management Research Symposium.* **Mount Saint Vincent University, Nova Scotia, 1988, pp. 2.14-2.46.**

Women are making a substantial impact on the employment market, both in terms of overall numbers as well as by appointment to male-dominated organizational roles. Research on women in leadership positions within organizations has concentrated on two main foci. Firstly, the identification of relevant individual and organizational characteristics and secondly, on the impact of these variables on the women in management role. This paper presents the findings from a series of studies in relation to these broad dimensions.

Ruble, T., Cohen, R., and Ruble, D. "Sex Stereotypes — Occupational Barriers for Women." *American Behavioral Scientist*, **vol. 27, no. 3, January/February 1984: pp. 339-356.**

The focus of this article is sex-stereotypes and how they create and maintain barriers for women in the workplace. A review of the existing research leads the authors to conclude that sex-stereotypes and occupational sex-typing reinforce one another and present hurdles at different stages of women's careers — at the decision making stage re: occupational choices, at the entry level and at the advancement and promotion stage within organizations. Biases are often subtle and at the evaluative stage may limit opportunities for career advancement. According to the authors, the possibility of bias seems to be most pronounced when performance information is ambiguous.

Russell, T. "Building the Foundations for Employment Equity: The Consumers Gas Experience." *Business Quarterly*, **vol. 52, no. 3, 1987/88: pp. 63-68.**

Consumers' Gas Employment Equity Program adopted in 1984 opted for a gradual approach to improving equity for women employees particularly in improving the representation of women in non-traditional jobs and in improving female representation in management. This article presents an overview of the process adopted by the company. Initial steps taken to prepare the ground for the equity initiative are identified and the specific initiatives that followed are detailed. The article concludes by highlighting the elements that appear crucial to the strategy's success. Included are sensitizing managers and presenting equity as an issue that must be managed; encouraging local initiative (as opposed to imposing a set of measures determined by head office); shifting the responsibility to line managers as quickly as possible; making managers accountable for the success of the program; giving women the tools to manage their career and recognizing that effecting a "fundamental change in corporate culture" will take time. The author is convinced that moving too quickly can be counter-productive.

Safarti, H., "La promotion de l'égalité de chances et de traitement en faveur des femmes dans la vie active: Quels problèmes? quelles perspectives?", *Travail et Société,* **vol. 10, no. 3, septembre 1985, p. 291-305.**

Cet article se veut un tour d'horizon de l'évolution général du travail féminin dans différentes régions du monde. L'auteure présente un aperçu des principales inégalités dont les femmes sont victimes notamment, la ségrégation sectorielle, la formation, la rémunération, les choix professionnels, la protection sociale et le chômage. En deuxième lieu, elle faits état des progrès réalisés sur le plan de la législation, de la jurisprudence et des conventions collectives, et des diverses politiques de promotion de l'égalité qui ont été mises en oeuvre depuis 1985. Quoique les résultats sont quand même "pas minces", l'auteure souligne que l'objectif d'égalité qui avait été fixé par les Nations Unies durant la Decennie pour les femmes est loin d'avoir été atteint.

Sales, A. et Bélanger, N., "Les femmes et l'inégalité d'accès aux postes de direction et d'encadrement", *Décideurs et gestionnaires,* **Québec, Éditeur officiel du Québec, 1985, p. 285-315.**

Ce chapitre décrit la situation des femmes dans les postes de direction dans le secteur privé et le secteur public du Québec et analyse leurs caractéristiques individuelles (âge, langue, revenue, état civil, éducation, etc...) et par la suite, leurs caractéristiques positionnelles. Les auteurs constatent que l'univers des décideurs et gestionnaires reste un monde masculin et que la situation des femmes cadres dans le secteur privé est très différente de celle des femmes cadres du secteur public. Les femmes du secteur public sont dans l'ensemble mieux placées dans la structure hiérarchique de leur organisation.

Sargent, Alice, G. *The Androgynous Manager.* **New York: AMACOM, 1981.**

A. Sargent looks at differences between the way men and women manage in most organizations. She concludes that neither, alone, provides an adequate model for management in this decade. The issue for women is not to imitate men. Rather, it is for women to adopt the best that men have to offer, and for men to do the same with the contributions that women make.

Schein, V.E. "The Relationship Between Sex Role Stereotypes and Requisite Management Characteristics." *The Journal of Applied Psychology*, vol. 57, no. 2, April 1973: pp. 95-100.

Researchers posed the hypothesis that successful middle managers are perceived to possess characteristics, attitudes and temperaments more commonly attributed to men than women. Results of a survey of 300 male middle managers confirms the hypothesis. Discusses implications for selection and promotion, a woman's self-image, and stereotypical perceptions of men and women among older managers.

Schein, V.E. "Relationships Between Sex Role Stereotypes and Requisite Management Characteristics Among Female Managers." *The Journal of Applied Psychology*, vol. 60, June 1975: pp. 340-344.

In a replication of a 1973 study of male middle managers, 167 female middle managers were surveyed to determine whether successful middle managers are perceived to possess characteristics, attitudes and temperaments more commonly ascribed to men than women. Results of the survey showed the author's hypothesis to be true, and they suggest that women in the early years of a career in management are especially apt to accept the masculine stereotype as more successful.

Schwartz, F.N. "Management Women and the New Facts of Life." *Harvard Business Review*, January-February 1989: pp. 65-76.

Schwartz states that employing women in management jobs is more expensive than employing men. Corporations, however, can reduce that cost greatly by changing their attitudes and being more flexible in order to retain their talented women in a very competitive market. Two separate groups of women should be identified and nurtured — "career primary" women, most of whom will be childless and will put their careers first and should therefore be given the same opportunities talented men are given and "child and family" women who wish to pursue careers while rearing their children. The author maintains that while these women are productive and committed, they are not likely to be upwardly mobile for a period of time. However, they are a valuable asset and should be supported in their need for flexibililty. The advantages and costs of part-time and shared employment are discussed and other family supports (parental leave for men, support for two-career and single-parent families during relocation) are identified. However good quality child care is identified as the most important element and companies are urged to get involved.

Schwartz, F. "The Controversy is Healthy." Reply to Letters to the Editor re: "Management Women and the New Facts of Life," *Harvard Business Review*, **May-June 1989.**

The author summarizes the main points of her controversial article and summarizes the negative reactions that her proposals have elicited. While arguing that in the long term women's interests could be sacrificed if difficult issues are denied rather than addressed now, the author goes on to underline three trends that she perceives as promising. Some companies are experimenting with flexible work arrangements at the managerial level, other companies are attempting to define company policies on maternity that serve both women and the organization's interests and thirdly, still others are recognizing the need to expand flexible policies to include men.

Many of the letters to the editor took exception to the author's description of two types of corporate women, calling it narrow, restrictive, simplistic and a contribution to barriers rather than to options. Others admonished her for not recognizing the "new facts of life", i.e., that men are now trying to balance work and family commitments. Sex discrimination is the cause of women's problems rather than women's multiple roles some argued and the "mommy track" is really the "mommy trap." Others described "third wave" companies that are based on flexible structures for both men and women and that don't support current corporate life and values at the "desired normalcy." Still others applauded the author's realistic view of the barriers women face and her "commonsense" ideas, arguing that the article can do much for the advancement of women.

Serdjenian, E., *L'égalité des chances ou les enjeux de la mixité*, **Paris, Les Éditions d'organisation, 1988.**

Dans un premier temps, l'auteure décrit l'évolution du rôle économique des femmes dans les pays européens, en particulier en France. La ségrégation des emplois (les fonctions productives et techniques sont réservées aux hommes, l'éducation, la santé et les services personnels restent féminisés) et la minorisation persistante des femmes sur le marché du travail sont discutées. La subordination familiale et économique des femmes amène l'auteure dans un deuxième temps à étudier comment les femmes vivent leur situation professionnelle. Dans un chapitre sur les contraintes, elle souligne le rôle de la maternité dans la carrière des femmes. Selon ses données la crainte de voir quitter les femmes lorsqu'elles se marient ou lorsqu'elles ont des enfants est la raison majeure citée par les employeurs pour expliquer pourquoi on n'embauche pas davantage de femmes. Par la suite, l'équilibre entre vie familale et vie professionnelle et le manque de disponibilité qu'on attribue aux femmes avec des enfants deviennent des contraintes à leur carrière. Elle étudie aussi la perception et l'image professionelles de la femme qu'ont les hommes et comment ceci est relié à ce qui bloque l'accès des femmes à certains postes et responsabilités. Dans une troisième partie elle compare les mesures d'égalité adoptées par certains pays européens, le Canada et les Etats-Unis et elle consacre un chapitre sur les étapes à suivre afin qu'une entreprise puisse appliquer des lois égalitaires. Une double action est proposée — une au niveau des programmes de personnel et une au niveau du personnel même.

Serdjenian, E., *Les femmes et l'égalité professionnelle,* **Paris, INSEP Editions.**

L'égalité professionnelle ne fait pas encore partie intégrante de la culture française selon l'auteure, bien qu'elle est inscrite dans la loi. Ce livre se veut un guide pratique pour les employeurs qui veulent pratiquer l'égalité des chances. En premier lieu, un diagnostic de la situation des femmes est nécessaire et l'auteure identifie les différentes phases d'une telle étude. Dans une deuxième partie, les discriminations directes et indirectes sont identifiées et les moyens d'action possibles sont décrits. Une troisième partie décrit la mise en place d'un programme d'égalité, y inclus une discussion sur la résistance et les stratégies possibles.

Shapiro, E.C., Haseltine, F.P., and Rowe, M.P. "Moving Up: Role Models, Mentors and the Patron System." *Sloan Management Review,* **vol. 19, 1978: pp. 51-58.**

Increasing effort, time, and money are being invested in projects for women. Many are intended to recruit and promote women in traditionally male professions, such as management, science, medicine, dentistry, engineering, and architecture. Much emphasis has been placed on "role models" and "mentors" as prerequisites for women's success. The authors examine these concepts and suggest (1) that role models are of limited effectiveness in assisting women to gain positions of leadership, authority, or power and (2) that mentors are at one end of a continuum of advisory/support relationships that facilitate access to such positions for the proteges involved. The authors conclude that careful consideration of this continuum will lead to better focused and more effective efforts directed at bringing women into positions of leadership and authority.

Simard, C., *L'administration contre les femmes: la reproduction des différences sexuelles dans la fonction publique canadienne,* **Montréal, Boréal Express, 1983.**

L'auteure fait l'historique des lois et des mesures restrictives dans la fonction publique fédérale qui ont désavantagé les femmes jusqu'à la fin des années soixante. Par la suite, elle décrit les années soixante-dix en faisant une étude détaillée du système du mérite et des structures et pratiques d'embauche, de promotion et de formation. Selon elle, le système ne sert qu'à consolider la position des personnes qui sont au départ favorisées, c'est-à-dire, les hommes. Un historique des attitudes et des pratiques discriminatoires des syndicats au sein de la fonction publique est aussi inclus. Elle termine par une revue des mesures égalitaristes aux Etats-Unis et au Canada et elle constate que la segrégation sexuelle par groupes occupationnels et par ministères existent toujours. Exception faite des progrès réalisés au sein des emplois de haute direction, ces mesures égalitaristes ont peu d'effets étant donné la rigidité de la séparation entre les emplois masculins et féminins.

Skinner, J. "Who's Changing Whom? Women, Management and Work Organization." in Coyle, A., and Skinner, J., *Women and Work — Positive Action for Change.* **Great Britain: Macmillan Education Ltd., 1988: pp. 152-169.**

Positive action and change must go beyond the individual women, the author contends, and include change in "organization culture, work processes and roles at work. "A summary of the different rationales for positive action is provided and the differences in focus on individual change versus organizational change are described. A discussion on the relationship of positive action to general trends in the management of work follows. Working patterns are changing it is argued and one outcome could be positive advancement for women. In the "here and now" however, women need positive women-only training opportunities, career guidance, survival knowledge and skills regarding the man-made corporate structure.

Slack, J.D. "Affirmative Action and City Managers: Attitudes Towards the Recruitment of Women." *Public Administration Review*, March/April 1987: pp. 199-206.

This article summarizes the results of a study on attitudes of 290 American municipal government officials to the use of affirmative action programs in the recruitment of women in the public sector over 55% of the city managers (93% of which were white males) supported the principle of affirmative action but the level of support was substantially less for some specific mechanisms designed to implement the principle (for example, special recruitment efforts, involvement of external groups in the hiring process, the use of targets and timetables).

Smeltzer, L.R., and Werbel, J.D. "Gender Differences in Managerial Communication: Fact of Folk-Linguistics?" *Journal of Business Communication*, vol. 23, no. 2, 1986: pp. 41-50.

There is a stereotype of women that holds that they demonstrate ineffective communication characteristics such as verbosity, constrained vocabulary and indirect requests.

A study of male and female MBA's was carried out to determine the validity of above stereotype. The study found no differences to exist in written communication between the male and female participants.

Spencer, A., and Podmore, D. *In a Man's World — Essays on Women in Male-dominated Professions.* London: Tavistock Publications, 1987.

As the title suggests, this book explores the experience of women in male-dominated professions. A constant theme is the notion of "discriminatory environments" for women where their careers are "shaped in detrimental ways as a result of their gender" and the notion of the "marginalization" of women. Of particular interest are two articles that deal with women in the British civil service (Walters, P., *Servants of the Crown* pp. 12-32; Homans H., *Man-made Myths; The Reality of Being a Woman Scientist in the NHS*, pp. 87-112). Walters argues that the organization and the culture of the British higher civil service is such that there is an expectation of total lifelong commitment to a career in which there is little room for differences and no room for "group" interests. Men and women are assessed differently for promotions and assignments Walter argues despite the systematization of evaluations. Men are assumed to be competent unless they prove otherwise while women need to establish their competence. Homans looks at managerial attitudes that affect opportunities for female scientists and identifies myths about women that the data do not substantiate, i.e., the myth of pregnancy and myths about natural aptitudes. Change is only possible, the author concludes, if women become more aware, if male attitudes to women change and if the organization of work itself is changed.

Spruell, G. "Making It, Big Time — Is it Really Tougher for Women?" *Training and Development Journal,* **August 1985: pp. 30-33.**

Two different points of view are discussed with regard to equal opportunity for women. Opponents of special efforts claim that if there are problems they are with individual women, i.e., their aspirations aren't high enough, they don't choose the "right" jobs (staff versus line jobs), they haven't been in the work force long enough to get to top management and reconciling family and career is just a question of organization. Those who support more formal assistance for women point to the subtle and intangible barriers facing women, i.e., conflicting views on appropriate behaviour, women's lack of visibility in organizations and the difficulty of reconciling family and career.

Stamp, G. "Some Observations on Career Paths of Women." *The Journal of Applied Behavioral Science,* **vol. 22, no. 4, 1986: pp. 385-396.**

This article seeks to contribute to a structural theory considering the connections among individual and organizational influences on career paths. Using stratified systems theory, the author develops a model of structural and individual development that integrates individuals' capabilities and organizations' requirements and defines work in terms of time frames for completing goals. A sample of 168 women managers and military officers from the United Kingdom and United States took part in semistructured interviews, and the resulting data are used to describe different types of career paths and consider the consequences of different types of potential. The author concludes that institutional barriers have different natures and impacts on the full realization of women's competence at different strata of organizations.

Statkus, R. *Intraorganizational Career Mobility: A Multifaceted Phenomenon.* **Research paper, Concordia University, March 1985.**

This study shows intraorganizational career mobility as a combination of individual factors and organizational factors. The rate of mobility is linked to individual factors, whereas the direction of mobility is more closely associated with the level of task interdependence and the managerial and autonomy career variables.

Stead, B.A. *Women in Management.* **New Jersey: Prentice-Hall, 1985.**

This book combines both research findings on women in management and practical advice on how to succeed. Of particular interest are the following articles:
- "Strategies for Helping Women Managers — or Anyone," by M.A. Lyles, (p. 16). This article reviews the barriers that stand in the way of women (socialization, sex-role stereotyping, lack of political awareness, tokenism) and outlines helping strategies including organizational strategies.
- "Sex Effects on Evaluation," by Nieva and Gutek (p. 111). This article focuses on the problem of sex bias in evaluation.
- "Implicit Stereotyping in Personnel Decisions," by K.A. Kovack (p. 149). Highlighted are the "unintentional subconscious sex stereotyping" that takes place every day.
- "Unforseen Business Barriers for Women," by G. Collins. Summarized are the results of a study on male and female managers that uncovers two subtle forms of sex discrimination related to promotional patterns and supervisory feedback. The "critical mass" theory, that is, as more women enter organizations "sexism and job discrimination will decline markedly as women occupy 15% of management positions and that at the 35% level an equal-opportunity balance will be achieved" is also questioned.
  Also, Chapter V includes a number of articles in networking.

Stewart, L.P., and Gundykunst, W.B. "Differential Factors Influencing the Hierarchical Level and Number of Promotions of Males and Females within an Organization." *Academy of Management Journal,* **vol. 25, no. 3, 1982.**

A study of perceptions of the promotion process for males and females within a large organization revealed that, after control of certain other factors, males had higher job grades than did females, although females had a greater number of promotions. This and other findings emphasize the need for a separate theory of career development for men and women.

Sutton, C.D., and Moore, K.K. "Executive Women — Twenty years later." *Harvard Business Review*, Sept.-Oct. 1985: p. 42.

A survey of 1,900 men and women, based on a duplicate survey done by HBR in 1965, shows that while male executives' attitudes have changed greatly over a twenty-year period, women still see resistance to their progress in the corporate world.

Swimmer G., Gollesch, D. "Affirmative Action for Women in the Federal Public Service." In *How Ottawa Spends, 1986-87: Tracking the Tories*, ed. Prince, M. Toronto: Methuan, 1986: pp. 208-249.

After presenting an overview of the representation of women in various occupational categories in 21 federal government departments and agencies, the authors examine specific areas such as the competition process, acting appointments, reclassifications, training and performance appraisals. They conclude that the "...federal government is currently a model employer..." and that the system is "...now generally equitable." However, they contend that for women as a group, the future is bleak given the Government's priority for fiscal restraint.

Symons, G. *Corporate Culture, Managerial Women and Organizational Change*. Paris: École Nationale d'Administration Publique, 1986.

This paper examines the "effects of the presence of managerial women in the corporate culture in organizations" — what does this presence change and to what extent do women conform to the corporate culture. The data were derived from a longitudinal study of 100 women managers in France, Quebec and English Canada. Women are described as a "force for change" both as an example for others and as a sponsor for other women. Barriers to advancement such as rigid initiation rites, blocked mobility, slower progression through the ranks and negative attitudes towards women are also noted. However, there are real constraints for change and the author anticipates that white women will modify the corporate culture, it will "neither (be) radical nor swift."

Symons, G.L., "La carrière! un vécu au féminin", *Gestion*, vol. 7, no. 3, septembre 1982, p. 16-21.

À partir de témoignages de 100 femmes gestionnaires au Canada et en France, l'auteure examine la perception qu'elles ont de leur situation et des défis et les contraintes de leur carrière en tant que femmes. Cette étude interculturelle met en relief des expériences communes liées à la situation de minoritaire des femmes. Cheminement de carrière, le parrainage, le statut de minoritaire, et la conciliation famille-carrière en sont les principaux thèmes.

Tarrab, G. et Simard, C., *Une gestion au féminin — nouvelles réalités*, Ottawa, Éditions G. Vermette Inc., 1986.

Ce livre est un résumé d'interviews avec 24 femmes gestionnaires du Québec. La carrière au féminin, les obstacles que les femmes rencontrent, le rapport des femmes au pouvoir, le style de gestion — telles sont les grandes questions examinées ici. L'introduction met en contexte la femme gestionnaire d'aujourd'hui, les obstacles qu'elle rencontre et l'importance de développer des réseaux de solidarité.

Taylor, A.L. "Why Women Managers are Bailing Out." *Fortune*, August 18, 1986: pp. 16-23.

An attempt to discover why many women MBAs from the class of '76 are leaving their corporate jobs ten years later to start their own businesses, work part-time or stay home. The author concludes that to keep women large organizations have to be more flexible, more hospitable and more equitable.

Taylor, P. "Women in Organizations: Structural Factors in Women's Work Patterns." In *Women Working: Theories and Facts in Perspective*, ed. Stronberg, A., and Harkess, S., California: Mayfield Publishing Co., 1988: pp. 167-182.

This article discusses both the formal and informal structure of organizations, how men and women are differentially affected by it and the consequences this has on the working lives of women. The basic premise of this article is that "the social structure of both the formal and informal organization is biased in favour of men's work and life experiences." Consequently, it is argued, the rules that are meant to facilitate work may actually exclude women, men are "disproportionately the supervisors and women the supervised" and men and women occupy different job ladders. As well, the informal organization that plays a crucial role in the recruiting and training of new entrants and in the selection of candidates for higher-level positions, excludes women. Organizational remedies are required to rectify this situation and the author recommends that strategies be aimed at both the formal and informal structures. Recommended strategies include job enrichment, "bridging" jobs, instituting equal pay for work of equal value and the development of women's networks.

Taylor, M.S., and Ilgen, D.R. "Sex Discrimination Against Women in Initial Placement Decisions: A Laboratory Investigation." *Academy of Management Journal*, **vol. 24, no. 4, 1981: pp. 859-865.**

An in-basket study revealed that both men and women held the view that female employees to a greater extent than new male managers are more suitable for routine, low-challenging positions than for stimulating, high-challenging ones. This is reduced after the person works with a competent, high-performing female holding a traditional male job.

Turcot, G., "Femmes et emplois: quatre enquêtes, un constat", *Relations*, **mai 1988, p. 116-119.**

Dans le contexte des prochaines négotiations collectives dans le secteur public au Québec, l'auteure fait ressortir les traits majeurs de quatre études sur la discrimination y inclus la discrimination salariale. Selon l'auteure, les conditions d'un véritable accès à l'égalité pour les femmes incluent l'élimination de la discrimination historique où la promotion est conjugé au salaire et à l'expérience, la mise en application du principe "à travail équivalent, un salaire égale", et la restructuration salariale du secteur public.

Vertz, L.L. "Women, Occupational Advancement and Mentoring: An Analysis of One Public Organization." *Public Administration Review*, **May/June 1985: pp. 415-423.**

This article is a case study of the obstacles to the career advancement of women throughout (as opposed to only women in management positions) the Internal Revenue Service (Milwaukee Districts Office). In addition to identifying career obstacles, some obstacles are discussed in the context of mentoring. If mentoring is adopted by an organization, it must be carried out in systematic fashion the author contends and five steps to assist in such an approach are recommended.

Wand, B. "Sex Differences in Educational Aspirations and Academic Performance in High Students." *Atlantis*, vol. 3, no. 1, 1977.

This study raises the question of which factors affect a girl's educational aspirations and academic planning and performance. Findings show that some of the attitudes held by the girls are even more traditional than those held by the boys.

Warner, R.L., and Steel, B.S. "Affirmative Action in Times of Fiscal Stress and Changing Value Priorities: The Case of Women in Policing." *Public Personnel Management*, vol. 18, no. 3, 1989: pp. 291-309.

Given that public sector affirmative action programs must contend with both political and economic trends, and given the advent of fiscal constraints facing many cities, the authors ask if it is "reasonable" to expect progress in the employment of women in non-traditional roles within municipal governments. Based on data gathered from 280 municipal police departments in major American cities over the period 1978 to 1987, the authors contended that the "above average utilization rates" for women are associated more with political variables than economic ones, i.e., budget conditions didn't significantly affect their utilization of women as police officers as much as political factors. The results suggest that having "women involved in the political structure benefits women in municipal employment."

Wente, M. "The Woman Who Never Was." *Canadian Business*, June 1985: p. 253.

The author asks why there are no women CEOs in Canada's Top 500 companies and summarizes the three most common explanations given to explain away this situation — women haven't been in the pipeline long enough to produce candidates for these jobs, women have to give men more time for their "comfort level" to adjust and women don't have the aggressiveness and commitment required for these jobs.

Williams, M.J. "Women Beat the Corporate Game." *Fortune*, September 12, 1988: pp. 128-138.

Successful female managers have not "feminized" the corporation by making it more aware of family concerns. In fact, according to the author, they have had to take on the values and life patterns of careerist men and to learn to play by the rules of the corporation. However, in spite of impressive gains in the middle management stream, women (and other minorities) are dropping out of large corporations at twice the rate of white males. Some employers are now coming to the conclusion that part of the problem may be the corporation itself and they have designed programs to retain and promote women. "Upward mobility" programs are designed to better equip women and give them more confidence by sharpening their managerial and quantitative skills and to encourage male managers to accept women by helping to change their attitudes or at least their behaviour. Other corporations have established upward mobility goals or quotas and some tie their managers bonuses to their progress in reaching these goals.

Willis, H., and Dodgson, J. "Mentoring of Canadian Women in Educational Administration." *The Canadian Administrator*, **vol. 25, no. 7, April 1986: pp. 1-6.**

The purpose of this research was to examine the influence of mentors on the career of Canadian women in a public-sector environment, i.e., in educational administration. Twenty-four female administrators from seven school systems across Canada were surveyed and 113 others responded to a questionnaire. Results indicate that although mentors had contributed substantially to the career success of the women inter-viewed, most of them were unaware at the time of the mentoring expe-rience that they in fact had a mentor. Those interviewed also expressed a great deal of ambivalence about institutionalizing the mentoring process. The authors conclude that many who have experienced men-toring believe that their mentors had an important influence on their careers. However, they note that a lack of mentoring did not prevent 41% of the respondents from entering the administrative ranks.

Wilson, S.J. *Women, the Family and the Economy.* **Toronto: McGraw Hill Ryerson Ltd., 1982.**

Central themes of this book are women's family roles, women's work and the relationship between women's domestic responsibilities and their secondary position in other social institutions. This relation-ship helps to explain the economic and social dependence that so many women experience. The women's movement has done a great deal to alter current perceptions, yet, this has not been accomplished without resistance.

Winn, C. "Affirmative Action for Women: More than a Case of Simple Justice." *Canadian Public Administration*, vol. 28, no. 1, 1985: pp. 24-46.

This article examines the affirmative action program for women in the Canadian federal civil service, examines the program's effects and considers alternative means of achieving the program's objectives. The author believes that the income gap between men and women should be equalized. However, affirmative action in the federal program is based on a "false picture" of the causes of the gender income gap. It is argued that the gender gap is not caused primarily by discrimination but by educational segregation and unequal family responsibilities. Affirmative action programs in the federal government are unjust to low-income women, low-status men and mothers who work at home. Proposed alternatives to such programs include reforms to income taxation, public pensions, education and job structures.